WHAT'S THE T?

JUNO DAWSON

T0018112

sourcebooks
fire

Copyright © 2022 by Juno Dawson
Cover design © 2022 by Sourcebooks
Design copyright © Hodder & Stoughton Limited, 2021. All rights reserved.
Illustrations © 2021 by Soofiya

Sourcebooks and the colophon are registered trademarks of Sourcebooks.

All rights reserved. No part of this book may be reproduced in any form or by
any electronic or mechanical means including information storage and retrieval
systems—except in the case of brief quotations embodied in critical articles or
reviews—without permission in writing from its publisher, Sourcebooks.

This publication is designed to provide accurate and authoritative information in regard
to the subject matter covered. It is sold with the understanding that the publisher is not
engaged in rendering legal, accounting, or other professional service. If legal advice
or other expert assistance is required, the services of a competent professional person
should be sought.—*From a Declaration of Principles Jointly Adopted by a Committee
of the American Bar Association and a Committee of Publishers and Associations*

This book is not intended as a substitute for medical advice from a qualified
physician. The intent of this book is to provide accurate general information in
regard to the subject matter covered. If medical advice or other expert help is
needed, the services of an appropriate medical professional should be sought.

The website addresses (URLs) included in this book were valid at the time
of going to press. However, it is possible that contents or addresses may
have changed since the publication of this book. No responsibility for any
such changes can be accepted by either the author or the publisher.

All brand names and product names used in this book are trademarks,
registered trademarks, or trade names of their respective holders. Sourcebooks
is not associated with any product or vendor in this book.

Published by Sourcebooks Fire, an imprint of Sourcebooks
P.O. Box 4410, Naperville, Illinois 60567-4410
(630) 961-3900
sourcebooks.com

Originally published in 2021 in Great Britain by Wren &
Rook, an imprint of Hachette Children's Group.

Names: Dawson, Juno (Young adult fiction writer), author.
Title: What's the T? / Juno Dawson.
Description: Naperville, Illinois : Sourcebooks Fire, [2022] | Originally
    published in 2021 in Great Britain by Wren & Rook. | Includes
    bibliographical references and index. | Audience: Ages 14 | Audience:
    Grades 10-12 | Summary: "Discover what it means to be a young
    transgender and/or nonbinary person in the twenty-first century in this
    frank and funny guide for teens"-- Provided by publisher.
Identifiers: LCCN 2021061192 (print) | LCCN 2021061193 (ebook)
Subjects: LCSH: Transgender people--Juvenile literature. | Transgender
    people--Identity--Juvenile literature. | Gender nonconformity--Juvenile
    literature. | Gender identity--Juvenile literature.
Classification: LCC HQ77.9 .D39 2022 (print) | LCC HQ77.9 (ebook) | DDC
    306.76/8--dc23/eng/20220107

Printed and bound in the United States of America.
VP 10 9 8 7 6 5 4 3 2 1

To whoever needs to hear this.

—J.D.

To Umber, Mika, and Zed

(I will always be thankful).

—S.

NOTE FOR PARENTS AND CAREGIVERS

Hello! If you're the parent or caregiver of a young transgender or nonbinary person, please turn to chapter 16 on page 291 where you'll find special advice just for you!

NOTE FOR ALL READERS

In this book, I've used *LGBTQ+*, *queer*, and *trans* as shorthand for the entire spectrum of sexual and gender identities. It's not the intention for anyone to feel excluded by those terms. Essentially, I mean anyone who isn't straight and/or cisgender.*

---

* For a definition of *cisgender*, turn to page 314.

Contents

PART ONE

ALL ABOUT IDENTITY

1

BECOMING ME

Hello, it's nice to meet you. My name is Juno Dawson, I'm an author from Brighton, UK, and I am a woman. Only one of those things was true to begin with.

When I was born a ridiculously long time ago, I was actually from Bradford, and I wasn't an author, because I was a tiny baby. Also, my parents called me *James*.

BUT I WAS ALWAYS A WOMAN.

It's true. I was. It just took me some time to figure it out.

You see, the doctor who oversaw my birth made a whoopsie. It really wasn't his fault. As far as he could tell from a quick scan of my body, I was a baby boy. What he couldn't have known all those years ago is that, for a tiny fraction of people globally, their eventual gender identity does *not* match their biological sex.

It's like a box of assorted chocolates: you can't always tell what's in the middle from looking at the outside.

It's super rare, but it does keep happening. It is a thing. We call it (at this moment in time) being **TRANSGENDER** or sometimes just **TRANS**. These days, it makes up the T in LGBTQ+.

> **L IS FOR LESBIAN**
> **G IS FOR GAY**
> **B IS FOR BISEXUAL**
> **T IS FOR TRANSGENDER**
> **Q IS FOR QUEER**

It took me almost thirty years to piece together the clues that I might be one of these mythological unicorn people I'd dimly heard about.

YES, I KNOW.
I'M BASICALLY A
FOSSIL PERSON.

You see, the 1990s, when I was a teenager, were a different time. For one thing, we didn't have the internet.

In some ways, without trolling, sexting, and Russian bots, the world was a nicer, simpler place, but it was also a less informed place.

When I was an infant, my parents had no access to information about trans children. As a child, I asked many, many times when I was going to "turn into a girl." I was told to stop being silly. When we played games out on the suburban cul-de-sac where I lived, I was *always* a girl character. I was Sheila from *Dungeons & Dragons* or Teela from *He-Man*. I had a Barbie doll that I used to make believe was Penelope Pitstop by constructing elaborate traps with string and toilet paper rolls. My parents were concerned about this "strange" behavior (even though it was actually perfectly natural for me), because they had no notion that this happens all the time, all over the world.

By the time I was ten or eleven years old, thoroughly shamed into silence and secrecy by pretty much every adult and peer in my world, I certainly wasn't telling anyone I wanted to be a girl. I was worried I'd get my head kicked in. But I did used to dream of the teenage girl I might magically turn into. I would lie in my cramped single bed each night and make a deal with God. *If I'm good, tomorrow can I be a girl?* And I could picture exactly the woman I'd grow into— I'd look like April O'Neil from *Teenage Mutant Ninja Turtles* or Peri from *Doctor Who*.

Sadly, my wishes didn't come true. At least *not yet*.

Later, as a queer teenager,* I didn't have access to the litany of amazing role models you'll read about in the Transgender Hall of Fame segments that separate each chapter of this book. I didn't have Laverne Cox or Janet Mock to aspire to. By 2005, the only trans person I'd ever really seen in the media was Nadia Almada, the winner of *Big Brother UK* season five. Even then, although I thought Nadia was great, I didn't connect her experience with mine, because in the *Big Brother* house, she didn't discuss her transition or childhood.

Now, you might know of me from the companion book to this one, *This Book Is Gay*, which I wrote in 2012 when I

---

* I use queer as shorthand for all LGBTQIA+ people because it marks us all out together as something other than straight or cisgender. I love that we, despite our occasional differences, march together as comrades. Also our queer identities may change over time, so "queer" captures me at any stage in my gorgey queer life.

was still known as James Dawson. While I was researching that title, I was very keen for it to be fully inclusive of all queer people. With this in mind, I set out to interview as many people as possible so the book wouldn't just be based on my experiences. I met lesbians, bi people, gay men from all walks of life, and yes, trans people.

It was during those research interviews that I started to meet people whose experiences were hauntingly like mine. They too had made deals with God in the night. They too had a very different vision of the adult they might grow into.

It hadn't even occurred to my clueless little brain that my whole life had been a **BIG FAT TRANSGENDER LIFE**. Right from day one. I lived as one person in public and as another, wholly different person in my head! How messed up is that? It was like having a girl twin who lived in another dimension. If I was in a women's clothing shop, I'd think, "This is what she'd buy." If I saw a cute haircut in a magazine, I'd think, "She'd get that hairdo." If I met a straight man, I'd think to myself, "She'd ask him out for coffee." I was living two lives. God, exhausting. Ain't no one got time for that.

As you can imagine, the life I was living in the flesh wasn't as much fun as the one I was having in my head. Everything I was doing as James was a bit half-assed. I really wanted to be someone else; I wanted to be *her*.

And so, one night in bed, I thought to myself, *Maybe*

this is what being trans is. Would that be so bad? I'd already been through the coming-out mill once as a teenager, and both I and my family had survived the ordeal. While living as a gay man, I'd been verbally abused, followed, even spat at in the street. Being trans couldn't be any worse. Or so I thought.

I was a grown-up, so I did a very grown-up thing and hired a therapist to talk through the many, many questions I had swimming around in my head. It was a confusing time. In lots of ways, it would have been *easier* to carry on being James and not rock the boat. I could have, but I had a huge fear that I was wasting my life. I keenly felt time slipping away. What's more, I met lots of other trans women who were living their best possible lives. I've spoken to some of them while writing this book. To be frank, I was jealous. *They get to be girls. Why can't I?*

This book is called *What's the T?* This is a phrase that origi-nated on New York City's ball circuit in the 1980s (the one you might have seen in *Paris Is Burning* or *Pose*), and it means "what's the truth?" I suppose that's what I finally learned in 2013: the truth about myself. Up until that point, I thought I *wanted* to be a girl when, in fact, I just *was* one. For all those years, I believed an error a doctor once told my parents.

Perhaps I should have asked my new trans friends how *hard* it was going to be, but regardless, I made the step and

CAME OUT! Again! Everyone was like "Whoa, twist!" and I was like "Yes, bitch. Psych!" I actually didn't say that, but people were super supportive.

My friends have been **AMAZING,** my readers and fans completely embraced me, and my father even agreed to film a documentary about it (although that's a different story).

So yes, for the last six years, I've been Juno and—honestly—happier than I have ever been in my entire life.

IF YOU WANT TO STOP READING AT THIS POINT, I'M TOTALLY DOWN FOR THAT.

That's because so often in the news, we see stories about transphobia, phony debates about trans lives, and brutal acts of violence committed against us.

You'd think, looking at the papers, that being trans is the worst-case scenario. If all you take from this book is that it's the **BEST THING I EVER DID,** I'm delighted, and I've done my job.

That said, I'm not here to sell you a transgender package.

It *really* doesn't work like that! God, if only, life would be much simpler. I don't know why *you're* reading this book.

- Maybe it was on a nice Pride display in a bookstore.
- Maybe it's in your school library and it has a nice cover.
- Maybe it's because trans issues are very *trendy* according to some papers.
- Maybe it's because you have a trans friend or family member and want to support them as much as you can. If that's you, thank you from the bottom of my heart. Your friend or relative will need all the help they can get.
- Or maybe it's because you have some questions about your gender.

Let's look at that last one. I think it's very normal for young adults to ask **BIG QUESTIONS**. All your life, someone (usually a parent or caregiver) has *told* you who you are and what you like. Now, all of a sudden, you have to answer big questions independently. What are your politics? What are your beliefs? What are your tastes in music, film, or food?

It seems really natural to me to assume that everyone will ask big questions of their identity too. It is the most fundamental thing about us—how we define ourselves at our core.

HOW DO WE PERCEIVE OURSELVES?

Ooh, it's a biggie. Adolescence is a particularly turbulent time for humans because we are already a mélange of hormones regardless of whether we're cis or trans. First love, first kiss, first pube: *everything* feels heightened. I should know. I went through puberty twice, and let me tell you, the second time—aged thirty-two—was no more fun than the first.

We all have a relationship with the notion of gender, because we were **ALL** labeled at birth. Even if you are inter-sex,* the doctor told your parents you were male or female, and from that moment on, a massive cartoon anvil of gender expectations landed on your head.

Our world is so disappointingly binary. The *bi* in *binary* means two, and we live in a world that likes to divide things into pairs. Sex and gender are no different: boy or girl, man or woman, male or female. From the first tiny blue or pink baby onesie you were dressed in, you had to decide how much you wanted to conform with certain stereotypes

---

* This will be more fully defined later.

THIS IS WHAT BOYS DO.

THIS IS WHAT GIRLS DO.

about boys or girls. Some girls feel very aligned to all things pink and sparkly, and some boys enjoy rough and tumble. Early problems arise when children of either gender *don't* adhere to stereotypes. They shouldn't, but ill-informed people might make comments—they might label girls as "tomboys" or boys as "effeminate."

Obviously, it's all a load of nonsense. There is categorically no "right" way to behave like a boy or behave like a girl, and I'd argue that medieval assumptions about gender are responsible for a great deal of awful in the world today—"oh, boys will be boys" or "that's not very ladylike."

SCREW THAT NOISE.

So while we're all deciding what kind of girl or boy we want to be, for trans people, it's that little bit harder. It goes so much deeper than what toys you want to play with or what clothes you want to wear. For me, it wasn't enough to "look like" a girl. I felt (with every fiber of my being) that I *was* a girl. If fate or nature or biology had been kinder, I would absolutely, one hundred percent have been born a girl with all the "typical" girl parts.

That didn't happen, unfortunately, and yes, I'm pretty bummed out about that. I had to take a very long and convoluted path before I could stand before you as a grown-ass woman. But I got there in the end. These days, I'm very proud to call myself a transgender woman. Gender: woman, subgroup: trans.

Some of you reading this book may well already be on the transgender express train, while some others may be thinking about whether to board. There will also be readers among you thinking that traditional, binary notions of gender don't apply to you personally. Never fear. This book also considers the ever-expanding lexicon humans are using to define or describe their relationship with that zany thing we call gender. So wherever you are on your journey, this is a book for you all.

Your gender is a **BIGGIE**. It will affect every part of your life for the rest of your life. From dating, sex, and relationships to your family and your body, your gender is central to everything you are and everything you do. This book can give you some pointers and guidance at a time when things might be confusing. To be honest, it's really a book of everything I wish I'd known when I was twelve. If I could go back in time (in a TARDIS, obv) and give myself this book, I like to think it would have helped my mental and physical well-being.

For the purposes of this book, I'm mostly addressing young gender-divergent people. We get talked *about* a lot, so I thought—for once—I'd talk *to* you.

Whether you're here as a trans person, a nonbinary person, or a cisgender ally,* you're all very welcome. Everyone's relationship with gender is individual, and **NONE** of us ever speak for a community. I *certainly* don't, so I've tried to make sure I've spoken to trans and/or nonbinary people who come from other minority backgrounds to ensure there's a range of diverse voices contained in these pages. As in *This Book Is Gay*, I haven't edited or "polished" their responses.

---

* Imma explain that later too. Don't worry.

I know I wish I'd spoken to a lot more trans people at the start of my journey to learn from their experience, so I've tried to gather as much practical advice as possible. But there's also a power in knowing that *however* you feel about your gender, **YOU ARE NOT ALONE**. Many thousands of people before you have gone through this and survived.

So grab yourself a cup of T (LOL) and settle down as we take a gentle riverboat tour through the modern transgender experience.

TRANSGENDER HALL OF FAME

JANET MOCK

USA · THE MULTITALENTED MOGUL

"I was born in what doctors proclaim is a boy's body. I had no choice in the assignment of my sex at birth... My genital reconstructive surgery did not make me a girl. I was always a girl."

Mock is a writer, producer, and director. The author of *Redefining Realness* and *Surpassing Certainty*, Mock became the first trans woman of color to write and direct for a television series when she went to work on *Pose*. She is one of the few trans women behind the camera, calling the shots in Hollywood.

2

WTF IS THE T IN LGBTQ+?

It's very simple.

A transgender person is someone who moves from one gender identity to another.

Gosh, that was easy.

I like to ask this question: have you ever moved to a new home? Now: have you ever moved genders? If the answer is yes, there's every chance you fall somewhere on the transgender spectrum.

Under the big, vast umbrella of transgender, some people might further define themselves as **TRANSSEXUAL**, **NONBINARY**, **GENDERFLUID**, **GENDERQUEER**, or **GENDER NONCONFORMING**. They all mean slightly different things that I'll go into more over the next few chapters.

The LGB section of LGBTQ+ stands for **LESBIAN**, **GAY**, and **BISEXUAL**. Those terms refer to sexuality, not gender, but we all belong to one larger community because a lot of the same people hate us. Plus, some trans people are *also* gay, lesbian, or bisexual.

The word **CISGENDER** simply means a person who *does* agree with the gender they were given at birth. The prefix *cis* is Latin for "on the side of." So the vast majority of people in the world are cisgender, even if they don't know the term.

All around the world and all across history, there is evidence of people changing their gender identity. We'll look more at the history of trans awareness in the next chapter, but it's enough to know this:

SOME PEOPLE CHANGE THEIR GENDER.

I think that's a really easy concept to wrap your head around.

- Sometimes a person who was told they were a girl realizes they're really a boy.
- Sometimes a person who was told they were a boy realizes they're really a girl.
- Sometimes people realize the terms *boy* or *girl* don't make sense for them as an individual and reject (or indeed, embrace) both.

The *trans* label encapsulates us all because we've all been brave enough to make that *change*. That's what unites us.

It's all quite straightforward. I'm really not sure what the fuss is about, to be honest. All over the world, a small group of people have made some decisions about their lives. Easy-peasy.

That said, you'd be forgiven for being very confused about the whole transgender thing. Since I wrote *This Book Is Gay* in 2012, there has been an unprecedented number of column inches in the press given over to stories about trans people. We find ourselves in the middle of a very unpleasant storm.

There are "debates," almost every week, on morning TV

shows about whether we should exist. A great many of these are based on falsehoods and opinions. Rarely have so few people been talked about so much. The press has very much treated trans and/or nonbinary people like we're something brand new, which simply isn't the case.

Either way, a lot of people have a lot of questions about trans people, and that's okay.

IT'S NOT TRANSPHOBIC TO HAVE QUESTIONS. IT'S TRANSPHOBIC TO HAVE CONCERNS.

One only has **CONCERNS** about bad things—global warming, bird flu, and corrupt politicians. Trans people are just people.

Never fear! I am on hand to help out and serve a delicious platter of jargon-free info so we can all move on with our lives. So, in the midst of so much chatter, what *is* the T? Let's take a look at some of the common "concerns" we often see in the media. I'll have a word with *those* people so you don't have to.

"BUT WHAT SHOULD I CALL THEM?"

Calm down, Carol. It's going to be fine. Here, have a brandy. The very simple answer is "their name." If someone introduces themselves as John, you should definitely call them John. That would surely be the most polite thing to do.

If what you mean is "What's the politically correct way to refer to a trans person?" well, the answer is in that question.

CALLING A TRANS PERSON *TRANS* IS FINE.

["BUT WHAT DOES THAT MEAN?"]

It's very simple, Alan. Broadly speaking, a trans person is **ANYONE WHO IDENTIFIES AS SOMETHING OTHER THAN THE GENDER THEY WERE GIVEN AT BIRTH.** You may have heard people speak about "gender dysphoria."

["IS THAT AVAILABLE AT IKEA?"]

No, Joan on Facebook, it's not. **GENDER DYSPHORIA** is something often experienced by trans and/or nonbinary people. It refers to the distress or anxiety caused when your gender identity doesn't match the sex you were assigned at birth.

"THERE ARE ONLY TWO GENDERS!"

Crikey! That escalated quickly. Be careful, @twogendersXXXY. You'll break your phone. That simply isn't true. The World Health Organization defines gender as "the characteristics of women, men, girls, and boys that are socially constructed. This includes norms, behaviors, and roles associated with being a woman, man, girl, or boy."*

Cultural norms (what is considered normal) vary wildly from country to country, meaning rules and customs regarding men and women shift too. Sometimes, things that we believe to be definitely true only exist that way because our little pocket of the world has deemed it so. A lot of our ethics, beliefs, and habits have been socially agreed upon or **CONSTRUCTED**. They are not real, solid things.

A good example is toilet paper. Obviously, toilet paper is *real*, but the way we approach it is socially constructed. No, stick with me. In some parts of the world, we wipe our butts with toilet paper and flush it down the toilet. In other places, you use tissue and put it in a little bin to be thrown

---

* World Health Organization, "Gender and Health," accessed November 1, 2021, https://www.who.int/health-topics/gender#tab=tab_1.

out in the garbage. In other places, toilets have little hoses to rinse off your b-hole. The "correct" way to clean your bum is a social construct that varies depending on where you are.

So as you can see, something that's a social construct cannot be **BINARY**. Something is binary when there are only two options, and clearly, in the world, there are more than two societies. An awful lot more than two and each with their own notions of masculinity and femininity.

Gender is what humans have decided is appropriate for men and women. Even the mere notions of "men" and "women" themselves are social constructs. At some point, ancient humans looked at our bodies and created the notion of binary gender based on our appearances, because this was way before DNA or a solid understanding of human biology. **MIND BLOWN**, right?

[**"THERE ARE TWOOOO GENDERRRSSS!"**]

Okay, hon, do you mean two *sexes*? The World Health Organization defines sex as "the biological characteristics that define humans as female or male. While these sets of biological characteristics are not mutually exclusive, as there are individuals who possess both, they tend to differentiate humans as males and females."* In humans, this means (usually) five characteristics:

GONADS:† Ovaries or testes.

SEX CHROMOSOMES: XX in females or XY in males.

LEVELS OF SEX HORMONES: Both male and female bodies produce testosterone and estrogen but in differing levels.

INTERNAL GENITALIA: The innie bits, the pipes and tubes and stuff.

EXTERNAL GENITALIA: The bits you can see on the outside. The penis and scrotum or labia and clitoris.

Obviously, all these bits and bobs are vital for making babies, but they're not the only things that matter. Because first, they are not the only things that define men and women. Second, it's not always so clear-cut. About 1 percent of live births are in some way intersex or possess sexual characteristics that don't fit the usual definition of male or female. And third, it should be clear that those five characteristics don't always equal a man or a woman.

---

* World Health Organization, "Gender and Human Rights," accessed November 1, 2021, https://www.who.int/reproductivehealth/topics/gender_rights/sexual_health/en/.
† What a hideous yet wonderful word.

Let's say a cisgender builder called Tim is going about his business when he has an accident at work and—oof—his external genitalia are torn clean off. Yes, ouch. Poor Tim. However, would we then say that Tim is no longer a man? No, of course not. If Tim still identifies as a dude, he is a dude. Fair? Yes. **REGARDLESS OF HIS BODY PARTS**, Tim is a man. This is how we define identity: **HOW WE FEEL ABOUT OURSELVES.**

"WOMEN HAVE VAGINAS!"

Yes, the vast majority do. No one is denying that. It is really important that we talk openly about genitals, because reproductive rights are super important. Abortion, female genital mutilation, endometriosis, ectopic pregnancies, and just *regular* pregnancies are highly politicized and have a bearing on how a person will navigate the **PATRIARCHY.**

"THE WHO? WHAT?"

I'm so glad you asked. A patriarchy is a culture in which men hold the majority of power, therefore creating a world that best suits men. Our world—pretty much the *whole* world—is a patriarchy. If you look at the people in power, they are mostly men.

Men, even now, still have freedoms that women do not. Men's bodies are not policed and debated like women's are. Men still earn more money than women and are more likely to receive an education. Girls are more likely to be married as children. Women still do the bulk of domestic chores, and millions of women do not have access to birth control.

So yes, primary sexual characteristics are hugely important, because they have a massive impact on our lives. This is something all cis women and all trans and/or nonbinary people very much have in common.

But gender is important too. How you are *perceived* matters.

Because I do not walk around in my **I AM TRANS** sandwich board, the world treats me as any old woman: I get all the same street and online sexual harassment that any woman would.

Sometimes trans men are

perceived as men or women. Sometimes nonbinary people are perceived as men or women too.

Being transgender in itself also affects how well a person thrives in the patriarchy. At times, I am treated specifically as a trans woman, so I get all the things cis women get plus a few salty side dishes, like online transphobia, street mockery, complications with my ID and paperwork, and so much more. Sometimes we're perceived as freaky weirdos with no rights at all. Identifying as trans and/or nonbinary is going to have a big impact on how well you can get by in a world run by men for men. It's partly to do with our bodies and partly to do with our identities—**THEY CAN'T BE SEPARATED.**

Clearly, identity and gender are really, really complicated, so let's simplify it:

NOT EVERYONE BORN WITH A VAGINA IS A GIRL, AND NOT EVERYONE BORN WITH A PENIS IS A BOY.

This is because of that important word *identity*. There can be a mismatch of your body (or how people perceive it)—something you had no say in whatsoever—and how you perceive yourself (or the labels you feel most comfortable with).

Life is a funny old lottery. Sometimes things don't go according to plan. I'm not suggesting being trans is an affliction or disability for a single second, and I can only speak from *my* experience, but I feel that had all gone according to plan, I'd have popped out with a tiny vagina.* But I didn't.

Hey ho, I got over it and realized my body does not define how I feel about myself and how I've always felt about myself.

As I got to know other trans people, it occurred to me that I'd never once thought about their genitals. Like, WHY WOULD I? Someone's privates are just that: private. They are their business and that of their sexual partners, alone. I recognized the trans men as men and the trans women as women without knowing or giving two shits about their privates or surgical history. And so should you.

Additionally, if we're going to be technical, this is the difference between a transsexual and a transgender person. Transsexual suggests an individual has taken steps to change their **PHYSICAL SEX**—not a prerequisite for being transgender **AT ALL**.

---

* Time for the standard I DO NOT SPEAK ON BEHALF OF ANYONE BUT MYSELF disclaimer.

We don't use *transsexual* as often these days (I sometimes do, because it sounds funnier if you're telling stories about being trans, tbh), because *transgender* or just *trans* does all the heavy lifting. Everyone knows what trans means, so it's just easier.

["IDENTITY ISN'T REAL."]

Every day, people identify as all sorts of things that have no relation to their biology: Christians, Jews, Muslims, addicts, godparents, husbands, wives, socialists, gays, lesbians, conservatives, pacifists, vegans...the list goes on and on. There is nothing more important than being free to identify however one feels. It is the very basis of human rights.

Are you British? American? Your national "identity" exists only because someone drew lines on maps.

Few identities are challenged in the way that **GENDER IDENTITY** has been over the last few years. Yes, identity is an abstract concept, but it's one we all undeniably have.

I was quite up front about it, only to be shamed into silence.

"YOU'RE ALL FREAKS!"

Linda, you need to chill; the pulsating vein in your head is gonna burst and cause a terrible mess. Although we don't have exact figures on precisely how many people are trans or nonbinary, we can estimate it's probably somewhere around 1.4 million people in the United States.[*] So taking the most liberal estimate, that gives us about 0.6 percent of the U.S. population.

Does that make us "freaks" or just a minority group? I think it's enough to not be "weird" or "strange" but too few to be a terrifying social contagion here to destroy the world. And it's not a new thing either. In chapter 3, I'll explore the rich and complex history of transgender people.

"WTF IS GENDER EXPRESSION?"

---

[*] Andrew R. Flores, Jody L. Herman, Gary J. Gates, and Taylor N. T. Brown, "How Many Adults Identify as Transgender in the United States?," UCLA Williams Institute School of Law, June 2016, https://williamsinstitute.law.ucla.edu/publications/trans-adults-united-states/.

Easy. That's how a person presents themselves to the world. Wherever we are in the world, we assign certain traits to genders. To me, that's a bit small-minded, but such is life. Certain clothes, hairstyles, and makeup have been assigned to men or women, and these **CULTURAL NORMS** vary over time and geography. Like, two hundred years ago, men were wearing the kind of massive powdered wigs RuPaul could only dream of. In South Asia or Scotland, it's perfectly normal for men to wear skirts.

Things that are very gendered in our world:

- Body hair
- Hair
- Names
- Clothes
- Toys
- Hobbies

Some trans people find solace in changing only their gender expression; they opt to wear or do things we *traditionally* assign to the opposite gender. Some trans people go one further and **SOCIALLY TRANSITION** by changing their names and documents, such as passports. Some trans people seek medical interventions or surgeries, altering elements of their physical sex.

I'll say this next sentence quite a lot, because it is very true:

THERE ARE INFINITE WAYS TO BE TRANS, AND THEY ARE ALL EQUALLY VALID.

Of course, it all very much matters, because those three things—your sex, your gender, and your gender expression—will absolutely affect how you exist in a very

sexist world that (almost universally) benefits men and
boys at a systemic level.

"DRESSING UP AS A WOMAN DOESN'T MAKE YOU ONE!"

Well, duh. There's no set way to dress as a woman—or
as a man, now that you mention it. Gendered clothing is
very much defined by where you are in time and space, but
this feels like a good place to discuss drag.

Despite my claim above that manhood and womanhood
can't be emulated with a few props and costumes, it only
takes a fake mustache or some hip pads to create a drag king
or queen, right? **WRONG.**

Drag is a very specific art form in which human bodies
are used as the canvas. There's a reason drag performers are sometimes called "gender illusionists": it's more
about creating a **CARICATURE** of masculinity or femininity.
It's a spoof, and not one intended to "convince" society
of any intention to live as a man or woman meaningfully.
Moreover, it's not a reflection of the performer's identity.

The key difference is what happens when the stage
costumes come *off*. A person's identity never truly begins

and ends with their apparel. It's an oldie but a goodie: **IT'S WHAT'S INSIDE THAT COUNTS.**

I perform in a queer cabaret collective called Club Silencio. Over the years, I've played Melania Trump, Rachael from *Blade Runner*, the angel Gabriel, and the Babadook's mum. When the costumes and OTT makeup come off, I'm still just Juno—a woman. Most days, you'll find me in actually quite masculine clothes—I favor jeans and T-shirts.

It's only when I'm at work engagements or on a red carpet that you'll see me in a dress. And they *are* costumes. Some days I play the role of serious author Juno or glamorous model Juno. But whatever I'm wearing, I am secure in the knowledge that I'm a woman.

Ro Robertson is another trans woman who works as a drag queen: Rococo Chanel.

A huge misconception about trans women is that we are "impersonating women," when the truth of the matter is we are just existing as ourselves. More realistically, a lot of trans women have probably spent a substantial period of their lives "impersonating men" to survive in a society that told us for so long—and to an extent continues to tell us—that we shouldn't or even don't exist. We are your sisters, friends, mothers, aunts; a different lived experience does not invalidate our womanhood.

I have been working as a drag performer since 2013, and when I started performing within the scene, I had not come out as trans, nor could I fully comprehend my identity at the time. From a young age, I had been discouraged from expressing femininity, so starting drag felt incredibly empowering. I began to understand and see my body in a new light after years of feeling uncomfortable in my skin. Eventually, seeing other trans women in the media who had evolved from drag to becoming their authentic selves (notably, thank you, Carmen Carrera), I was hit like a ton of bricks and realized what was making me so unhappy. I still remember the exact spot I was standing when I understood and came to peace with who I truly was.

Although drag undoubtedly helped propel the understanding of my gender, it has always been much more to me than "female impersonation." Drag is a wonderful vehicle and platform with which to explore different characters and ideas and is, of course, also a job. When the work is done, whether I've spent the evening as a black-and-white movie star, a clown, or a pig, when I get home and the drag comes off, I am just Ro: a softly spoken, introverted woman, a leap from the larger-than-life characters I'd brought to the club. Drag is a persona, a mask. To be myself, I don't have to wear one.

Ro Robertson, a.k.a. Rococo Chanel

"BUT HOW DO YOU KNOW THAT YOU'RE TRANS?"

Let me flip that one right back around, Jeff. How do you *know* you're a man? Pretty much it's because you were *told* so by a doctor or your parents or society.

Mind blown, right?

Because in the United States, 99.4 percent of us are in agreement with the gender we are assigned at birth, this labeling doesn't bother most people. It's up to each of us to make peace with our gender. It's a wholly personal experience. Unless you are a body-hopping alien life-form,* we have no way to live as someone else. As such, we cannot say there is one definitive way to "feel like a girl" or "feel like a boy."

For me—and lots of trans girls—I was told (A LOT) that I was a boy, but I always felt a great unease with that, which was dysphoria in action. When I was little, I was actually a bit bewildered that the rest of the world didn't perceive something that I thought was abundantly obvious:

---

* You should totally read *Every Day* by David Levithan, btw.

Moreover, with a bit of hindsight, I think a key difference between myself and cisgender kids is that when I imagined the future, I very clearly pictured a woman. I used to picture myself as lots of things: a plucky reporter, a flight attendant, a *Doctor Who* companion, but invariably, they were always women.

There was no future for me as a man.

So I guess that's *how I know*. What did I want to be when I grew up? Simple: a woman.

But don't just take my word for it. I'm so lucky in that I know some of the coolest trans and nonbinary people out there. How did they know?

I was around three when I really knew and felt I was a boy. I knew I was male and found it weird being called or referred to as a girl. I guess I've always felt that I've known who I've been, yet gender was a label that was placed on me, or how I was defined, for the benefit of ticking a box or to be categorized. What I was told I was isn't who I am, and I feel my gender is more accurately represented as I am now.

Leng Montgomery, inclusion manager

The simple answer is that I socially and medically transitioned, and it's literally only improved my life. And I've never regretted it. A few years ago, I'd have panics like, *What if you're not trans? You've just convinced yourself and made it all up?* But now it's easier to say—even if I did wake up and decide to be trans one day in 2014—that it's actually been a long enough time now, and my life is substantially better than pretty much any of it before that point. I know for some people, "being trans" is more of an identity they feel from a young age and that you don't have to transition to be trans. But in my case, I do see being trans as a series of actions and decisions I took. I have taken them. And I've never regretted any of them. So that's how I know I am trans.

Shon Faye, author and journalist

I think the moment I knew for sure was when someone random "mistook" me for a man and I just felt...right. For the first time. I believe the proper name for it is "gender euphoria."

Jay Hulme, poet

At the end of the day, whenever we discuss feelings, we are dealing with something quite abstract and very hard to put into words. Try describing joy or hope, and I'm sure you'd struggle too. It is very hard for trans and nonbinary people to explain how they know, but they *do*.

It just took me a really long time to put my finger on it.

Like Shon says, I too have never looked back. As we'll learn, being trans or nonbinary is far from easy, but my life now feels like mine. I'm no longer pretending or trying to please anyone else. This is who I am.

I think we can all agree that the most basic—but most frustrating—advice you're ever given is "be yourself." It's much easier said than done.

"WHAT IF YOU CHANGE YOUR MIND?"

Being trans is such hard work, I doubt anyone is going to put themselves through the rigmarole of coming out if they didn't truly believe it was the right course of action. Despite what you may have read, being trans isn't a trendy whim one embarks on because you like Hari Nef's hair. Transitioning takes years and years and years and never really finishes.

While I'm but one example, I did about twenty-eight years of soul-searching before I "suddenly" started my transition. Finding out someone *else* is transgender may well be surprising, but it doesn't mean it's out of the blue for them.

Moreover, if someone does come out as transgender and later decides that's not the right journey for them, I'm inclined to say "so what?" The whole point of me contacting lots of other trans and nonbinary people is to highlight that no two of us are the same. There isn't a one-size-fits-all "journey" to take. I'll say it again:

THERE ARE INFINITE WAYS TO BE TRANS, AND THEY ARE ALL EQUALLY VALID.

You have to find your gender sweet spot. Each individual gender-nonconforming person has to decide how to live their individual life, and yes, that will probably include changing their mind many, many times. Everyone else on the planet changes their mind a hundred times a day and isn't called out for it. Some people drift in and out of faiths, diets, and career aspirations.

Trans people are no different. Figuring out something as profound as gender takes years, not weeks, and over that time, it's perfectly fine to go back and forth until you find that sweet spot where you finally feel comfortable in your own skin. Trans people may have a slightly complicated relationship with sex and/or gender, and this may have a bearing on their gender expression.

The press makes an awful lot about people who "detransition," but they make up a *minuscule* percentage of trans people overall. Some studies measure "regret rates" after surgery, and other types of surgery have far higher regret rates than gender-affirming surgeries. For example, *cisgender* people are far more likely—statistically—to regret cosmetic surgeries (i.e., boob jobs, etc.) than trans people do their gender-affirming surgeries.*

Finally, even if every other trans person in the world suddenly detransitioned, I can tell you now, categorically, that I wouldn't. And my experience would be just as valid. The few people who've turned their backs on formal social or medical transition **MUST NOT** be used to call into question the sanity of the many, many millions more transgender people who have not. In my mind, they haven't detransitioned. It's just that their path toward their gender sweet spot is different from mine.

I'm speaking for myself, but never, ever has a sinister surgeon dragged me kicking and screaming into an operating room. I'm not sure that happens. As a consenting adult, I opted for some medical interventions (not to mention paid through the nose for my nose). That was my choice.

"BUT SURGERIES ARE IRREVERSIBLE!"

---

* And clearly not all trans and/or nonbinary people want surgeries in any case. Liam Knox, "Media's 'Detransition' Narrative Is Fueling Misconception, Trans Advocates Say," NBC News, December 19, 2019, https://www.nbcnews.com/feature/nbc-out/media-s-detransition-narrative-fueling-misconceptions-trans-advocates-say-n1102686.

Surgeries are, for the most part, irreversible but—and I've lost count of how many times I've said this—**TRANS YOUTH DO NOT GET SURGERIES.**† So what we're dealing with is adults making choices about their bodies. Is there a similar outcry over cisgender adults who get boob jobs, nose jobs, tattoos, face-lifts, and Botox? No, of course there isn't, because the furor you've read about trans surgeries is written by people who hate trans people. Portraying trans people as confused or misguided simpletons who've been brainwashed by some almighty "trans cult" and "mutilated" themselves is one of the more hilarious myths spread about transgender people.

You may have read about so-called **PUBERTY BLOCKERS.** This is a treatment designed to pause the onset of puberty. This medicine is given to cisgender children who experience very early puberty and cis women with heavy periods or endometriosis. However, in trans youth, it is sometimes prescribed at the onset of puberty to delay adult sex characteristics developing. Basically, they press Pause until adult treatment begins at sixteen.‡ If you stop taking them, you hit Play again, and the body enters into puberty. There's a lot more on this treatment later in the book.

---

† Globally, the age from which gender-affirming surgery can take place varies slightly, but it is usually eighteen years old.

‡ In the UK. Exact ages vary globally.

It really is about **BODILY AUTONOMY**. As should be the case for all human beings, we should be able to choose the destiny of our own flesh and blood. For some of us, that entails surgery. For others, it does not. Having surgery doesn't make you any more or less trans than someone who doesn't.

That's before we even get started on the cost of surgeries. Medical treatment expenses can add up to $100,000, and they're often not covered by health insurance in the United States.* So again, it's hardly the same as impulse-buying Haribo at the grocery store, is it?

"I AM NOT CISGENDER!"

Statistically speaking, you probably are, bbz. **Cisgender** simply means you're not trans, and you agree with the gender you were assigned at birth. About 99.4 percent of people in the United States are cisgender.

The term *cisgender* was likely first used by German sexologist, physician, and sociologist Volkmar Sigusch in

---

* Benji Jones, "The Staggering Costs of Being Transgender in the US, Where Even Patients with Health Insurance Can Face Six-Figure Bills," *Business Insider,* July 10, 2019, https://www.businessinsider.com/transgender-medical-care-surgery-expensive-2019-6.

the 1990s and then more explicitly by sociologists Kristen Schilt and Laurel Westbrook in 2009. So it's hardly newfangled. As academic conversations about trans people have widened over the last century, it certainly became necessary to have a term to describe the opposite of transgender, or else we were left only with the clunky "nontrans" or, worse, "normal."

I do not feel abnormal. It felt much more abnormal for me to describe myself as a boy or man. It felt like wearing an itchy wool shirt. To me, being Juno feels very normal indeed. I'm much more "normal" this way, so describing cis people as such really fails to distinguish us.

Also, being cisgender, white, straight, and nondisabled shouldn't be the default. Describing those attributes as "normal" is bullshit.

The way I see it, everyone has their biological sex, their gender, and their gender expression. These three things can intersect in all kinds of unique ways and different combinations. When I use the term *cis* to describe myself, I'm indicating that my gender matches my biological sex—i.e., I am a woman with a female body.

Using the term *cis* is one of the best ways to show solidarity with the trans and nonbinary community. It indicates that the world is not divided into "normal" and "freakish" but rather a majority whose gender and sex happen to align and a minority for whom they do not.

It's also a way of teaching people that what they see doesn't necessarily paint a comprehensive picture. Just because I am feminine in my gender expression does not mean you can assume I'm cis—I have to give you that information. It's the same reason I support organizations who ask all their employees or members to put their preferred pronouns on their email signatures.

Whenever we have an archetype we defer to when we imagine a person—whether that is white, straight, male, able-bodied, or cis—it results in people who don't conform to that archetype being marginalized. As a mental health campaigner, I know belonging is a key psychological human need and want to do everything I can to create an environment where nothing is assumed so that everyone feels that they belong.

Finally, using the term *cis* is a way for me to indicate that I recognize my own privilege, because life is undoubtedly easier right now for people whose sex and gender align.

Natasha Devon, campaigner, author,

and radio presenter

As Natasha so eloquently says, using the term *cisgender* (without being a weenie about it) is the easiest way you can show your support of the trans community.

When cis people are resistant to being called cis, I'm guessing it either comes from outright transphobia or a discomfort with being labeled.

If you are cis and straight and white and nondisabled, I imagine you're not used to being labeled. Hon, you get used to it. It isn't fair that our society treats straight, white, cisgender, nondisabled people as **THE NORM**. If people of color, LGBTQ+ people, and people with disabilities can acclimatize to those labels, then you sure can handle a label that speaks only of luck and good fortune.

Some people don't like "cisgender" simply because they hate trans people and want to erase us from the lexicon. More on hatred and transphobia later.

"WELL, I'M NOT USING IT. I DON'T CARE."

In that case, Bob, you are a weenie, and I'm done talking to you. I have politely answered all your questions, but I see you didn't come to this conversation out of willingness to learn, so I'm going to go watch *The Great British Baking Show* and cuddle my dog. Boy, bye.

LET'S RECAP!

TRANSGENDER

There are a gazillion ways to be trans, but pretty much all of them feature a person identifying as a gender different from the one they were given at birth.

CISGENDER

Someone who's A-OK with the gender they were given at birth.

TRANSGENDER HALL OF FAME

AYLA HOLDOM

UK · THE HELICOPTER HEROINE

"It is my hope that [better visibility] will mean young people will shake off the confines that have plagued past generations and forge new paths that don't necessarily conform to traditional standards. For trans people, that means recognizing, accepting, and living who you are without feeling like you have to change for others."

Holdom was the first and is still the only female helicopter pilot in the UK police force. She campaigns for better representation of trans people in the media with the awareness group All About Trans.

3
A BRIEF HISTORY OF TRANS

One of the most persistent myths about the trans and nonbinary communities is that being gender variant is a brand-new fad invented by Caitlyn Jenner in 2015. This *clearly* is not the case, but the accusation is used to undermine or belittle us. It all adds to the general vibe that we are "not real."

Trans people have always been here. You can find evidence of our existence throughout history, and there is abundant anthropological evidence (right up to the present) that we've been present in human societies around the world. Indeed, in many parts of the world, trans people have been historically revered—at least until our Western ancestors turned up to invade, exploit, and teach indigenous peoples our hang-ups about sex and what counts as natural.

Christine Burns, MBE, author of
***Trans Britain*, and historian**

Knowledge is power, and I think it's wise to arm ourselves with facts and figures when ill-informed or bigoted people accuse us of "being trendy." It's frustrating though, because literally no straight or cisgender person has to go to the trouble of learning how and why they came to privilege and supremacy, but there you go.

I now present a quick guide to transgender history.

LANGUAGE IS KEY

Okay, the first issue is that the term *transgender* is fairly recent in the grand scheme of things. It was first used in *roughly* 1965 by American psychiatrist John F. Oliven, who noted that *transsexual* didn't quite work because not all trans people want to alter their physical sex.

Transsexual was coined around the 1920s, when Dr. Magnus Hirschfeld was doing pioneering work—he is thought to have performed the first gender reassignment surgeries. He ran the famous Institute for Sexual Science outside Berlin, Germany, until the Nazis seized control of it during their rise to power.

Transsexual has somewhat fallen out of fashion over the last twenty years or so, although it is still occasionally used to describe a subset of trans people who do opt for surgeries and/or modify their sex. Instead, *transgender* operates as an umbrella term for *anyone* moving between traditional notions of male and female.

People still sometimes use the acronyms FtM (female to male) and MtF (male to female) to describe trans men and trans women. Doctors use these terms in their notes today, as it's not always instantly obvious what direction a trans person's journey is going in, and at the end of the day, your doctor needs to know!

However, in the 1990s and early 2000s, there was a general move away from the FtM or MtF monikers, as these terms only consolidated very binary, rigid, and limited grounds on which a person could transition. They left nonbinary people (who wouldn't chime with M or F) out in the cold.

Presently—because language will continue to evolve, as it always does—it's usually the case that transgender people refer to themselves as a trans man or a trans woman. Nonbinary or genderqueer people may well refer to themselves as neither, as I'll explore in the next chapter.

I am not a fan of the perplexing *transman* or *transwoman*. Yes, that space makes all the difference. I am a woman who happens to be trans. I am also a white woman, but no one would ever say I was a whitewoman, would they? You often see transphobic people using transwoman or transman because it's their way of not having to admit trans women are women and trans men are men. It *others* us, makes us some different species, makes us alien.

PRE-1920

Just because Hirschfeld coined the *word* transsexual, that certainly doesn't mean he invented the notion. After all, he was a doctor simply reporting a phenomenon he observed in his patients. So while they certainly wouldn't have used the word *transgender*, there have almost certainly been gender-variant people knocking about for as long as history has been recorded.

First up, we must acknowledge that history is largely written by the monsters, so much of what we know about gender in the past has been informed by European colonization and the eradication of indigenous people who didn't have binary notions of gender in the first place. Thankfully, some of those traditions endure today, and I'll explore them further in the next chapter.

What can we learn from historical evidence? Art discovered in Europe from around nine thousand years ago depicts genderless characters wearing both male and female clothing. A five-thousand-year-old burial site near modern-day Prague contained a "male" skeleton dressed in "female" clothes and adorned with items you'd only bury

alongside a woman. Alas, much of this historical evidence is, well, buried in conversations about our culture and past.

In ancient Egypt, pictures of goddesses are sometimes depicted with penises, and in "The Tale of the Two Brothers," a character called Bata removes his penis and tells his wife, "I am a woman like you." In ancient Rome, there was a sect of priests known as the Galli who worshipped the goddess Cybele and her consort Attis, occasionally castrating themselves and referring to themselves as women. Also in ancient Rome, the emperor Elagabalus preferred being called "lady" and wore wigs and makeup. Elagabalus's most enduring relationship was with a chariot driver, who they referred to as their "husband."

In medieval times, Eleanor Rykener was a sex worker who presented exclusively as a woman despite seemingly being born male. By all accounts, it seems she lived fully as a woman and may also have been bisexual. In the eighteenth century, the French diplomat the Chevalier d'Éon presented as a man initially but then later in life entirely as a woman, leading many to think of them as transgender or possibly intersex. The nineteenth century saw a fleet of people who'd been assigned female at birth becoming men to join the military. Notable examples include James Barry, an Irish surgeon, and Albert Cashier, who fought in the Civil War and "lived as a man" for at least fifty years.

In some ways, I imagine the era before medical transitions was a simpler time. Granted, you had zero rights or legal protections, but it seems to me that all through history, people were quietly transitioning and living their best possible lives. To be clear, they would not have used the term *transgender*—they were just men or women, and there's something pleasingly straightforward about that.

These examples provide evidence aplenty that transgender people's existence has *never* impacted on the rights or well-being of cisgender people.

EARLY PIONEERS

The advent of the twentieth century saw what feels like the formalization of the process that we now call **TRANSITIONING**. This probably isn't a coincidence: advancements in medical science, photography and television, air travel, and print media almost certainly acted as catalysts toward a greater understanding of trans issues—and of course dissemination of the term itself.

Without the following people, I think it's fair to say, we simply wouldn't be where we are now. Without the courage of these people, we wouldn't have the (admittedly still limited) rights we have today.

KARL M. BAER
1885–1956

In 1906, Baer became one of the first people to undergo sex reassignment and achieved a legal change of gender by receiving a new birth certificate. Baer worked closely with Magnus Hirschfeld to develop Hirschfeld's understanding of the trans experience, so Baer was utterly pivotal in history.

LUCY HICKS ANDERSON
1886–1954

Hicks Anderson knew from a very young age that she was a girl and, with the support of her parents, always "lived as a girl." Issues only arose when her second husband accused her of perjury for lying about her gender on a marriage license. Legal issues were to plague trans people throughout the century, eventually leading to the introduction of laws to protect us.

ALAN L. HART
1890–1962

An American scientist, Hart underwent his medical transition from 1917 to 1918 and was able to maintain a career in science. He went on to develop a pioneering system for using X-rays to detect tuberculosis. This innovation went on to save countless lives.

DORA RICHTER
1891–1933

Richter is thought to have been the first trans woman to undergo a vaginoplasty, though records of this groundbreaking work were lost during Nazi raids on Hirschfeld's institute. Richter worked as a maid at the clinic, and it's assumed she was killed during the raids.

LILI ELBE
1882–1931

Although much about her life is conjecture, since Elbe was another of Hirschfeld's patients, we do know that Elbe underwent sex reassignment surgery and died of postoperative complications. Her legend was consolidated by the Hollywood movie *The Danish Girl*.

BILLY TIPTON
1914–1989

This talented jazz musician was only outed as a transgender man after he died. Even his wives and adopted children assumed Tipton was cisgender. Tipton is further proof that trans people have been living, working, and thriving for decades. It is a shame to me that the times meant he had to conceal his truth.

MICHAEL DILLON
1915–1962

This British physician is best known as being possibly the first trans man to undergo a phalloplasty operation, but it vexes me greatly that so many trans people are remembered only for their surgically modified genitals. It's also worth noting that Dillon was the first white European man to be ordained as a Buddhist monk.

CHRISTINE JORGENSEN
1926–1989

Jorgensen is remembered for being perhaps the first trans media sensation, the Laverne Cox of her time. The former American GI was received well by the tabloid press when she publicly came out in 1952.

JAN MORRIS
1926–2020

Morris, a celebrated travel writer and historian, transitioned in the early 1970s and detailed her experience in her autobiography, *Conundrum*. She was treated kindly by the press—another example of how the media tone around trans people has changed over the last twenty years or so. Morris had to travel to Morocco for surgery because she wouldn't divorce her wife to do so legally in the UK.

APRIL ASHLEY
b. 1935

In contrast to Christine Jorgensen's experience in the American press, Ashley—a successful model—was outed by the *Sunday People* tabloid in 1961. There followed a messy marriage annulment and court case when her husband, who knew she was trans, claimed she had deceived him.

MARSHA P. JOHNSON and SYLVIA RIVERA
1945–1992 and 1951–2002

If we know one thing about history, it's that it's too often written by privileged (and white) hands. We will never know how many trans people of color struggled through history, because their stories weren't being reported or recorded in the same way that, say, beautiful, blond Christine Jorgensen's was. This pair—regardless of whether they identified as transgender, genderqueer, or gender nonconforming—are perhaps best known for their legendary involvement in the Stonewall riots of 1969, which essentially triggered the LGBTQ+ rights movement in the United States. Together, Johnson and Rivera—both people of color, both at times sex workers and people who experienced homelessness— formed Street Transvestite Action Revolutionaries (STAR) to protect LGBTQ+ homeless youth in New York. At one point, gay and lesbian activists distanced themselves from the outspoken Johnson and Rivera for making them "look bad," which hints at the way gender-nonconforming people are marginalized within the LGBTQ+ community. Yes, even today, there are some naysayers who think trans rights have nothing to do with gay rights despite trailblazers like Johnson and Rivera. Johnson was found dead in 1992, a fate that has sadly befallen many Black trans women, and it's only recently that the NYPD has started to treat her death as a potential murder.

RECOGNITION

What should be very clear from the cases above is that, throughout the twentieth century, a discreet state of being that we now call "being trans" had become a very definite thing. However, at this point, it was still defined in medical terms. Transition was a process that took you from A to B, usually under the guidance of medical professionals.

What was far less well defined was what happened *afterward*. As we saw with April Ashley, trans people were on very thin ice, legally speaking. Her marriage was annulled because, in the eyes of the law, she was a man.

With no laws in place beyond what we could and couldn't do medically, trans people were uniquely vulnerable in society. All that was to change thanks to the curious case of a bus driver in the United Kingdom wanting to claim her pension.

Christine Goodwin was that bus driver, and since she had medically transitioned some twelve years before, she felt she was entitled to receive her state pension at the same time as any other female bus driver. Back then, in the UK, women retired earlier than men, so Goodwin only felt it fair she should be treated like any other woman.

Alongside another anonymous trans person, Goodwin took her case to the European Court of Human Rights to petition for her name to be changed on her birth certificate and won. This all meant the UK government *had* to act and introduce legislation.

In 2004, the Gender Recognition Act was passed, which allows trans people—under very strict conditions—to apply for legal recognition and obtain a gender recognition certificate and a new birth certificate expressing their correct gender. It was a huge step forward and, at the time, was an innovative piece of legislation.*

Christine Burns, MBE, is one of those people to whom all trans people in the United Kingdom owe a debt of gratitude. Working with a group called Press for Change, Burns and Stephen Whittle, OBE, a trans man, campaigned tirelessly to achieve legal rights for trans people and were on the panel that advised the government on the formulation of the Gender Recognition Act. I asked Burns how things have changed during her long career as an activist.

Before the 1960s, people seeking to change their gender permanently had mainly solitary stories and, although figures of intrigue, were largely left alone, as they wished to be. All that changed with a sudden surge of press interest in the mid-1950s, when trans people were pursued like quarry to make scandalous copy for the Sunday

* There is more information about trans people and the law in chapter 13.

tabloids. In turn, this outside pressure encouraged trans people to try and organize to support one another. In a very real sense, the beginning of trans people coming together—the creation of what we might call a "community"—can be seen as a reaction to the unfairness of what the press were doing.

That external threat was cemented further in 1970, when the decision of a divorce case involving model and socialite April Ashley actively took rights away from trans people as a group. Until then, although trans people's rights weren't explicit in law, there was plenty of informal wiggle room to enable people to marry and hold down jobs. The divorce decision took that away. It was designed to prevent any other trans woman, like April, from marrying a man. That decision sowed the seeds for a great deal more marginalization that then followed. This is an unusual aspect of the trans rights struggle: it didn't begin with us always having been deeply discriminated against. The discrimination only really got started once we got ourselves noticed in a way the establishment didn't like.

Everything about the outcome of the April Ashley case has the feel of a brutal smackdown. In the mid-1980s, along came Mark—a quiet, polite, but incredibly brave and determined trans man—who had had enough and decided he would appeal to the law. The story of Mark Rees and the case he took all the way to the European Court of Human Rights was a turning point.* The story really deserves to be made into a film one day. He lost the case as it happens, but he showed my generation the way forward. There was a way to get people to listen to us—through the courts. Our plight was the very epitome of what human rights are about. And the evidence was blatant and consistent—so consistent, in fact, that it was essentially the same evidence of the disadvantages we suffered through not being legally recognized for who we are.

Once a way forward presented itself, it didn't take long for a group of committed volunteers to come together to campaign. Press for Change—a rallying cry if there ever was—began in a Westminster tea shop on February 27, 1992. Ten years later, in July 2002, the latest case brought by trans people to the European Court of Human Rights was successful. Along the way, Press for Change had already won other essential protections and earned enough credibility with lawmakers and civil servants to be chosen as the partners to help them frame what became the original Gender Recognition Act 2004.

Opponents of trans people often behave as though trans people are a novelty—a fad born out of Western decadence. They couldn't be more wrong. We've always been here. Our path to the present day began with searing injustice. It moved forward because we found

---

* In 1986, Mark Rees went to the Court of Human Rights because he wanted to be ordained as a priest. At the time, women could not become priests, and Mark, incorrectly, was believed to be female.

a way to change our world and we hung in there. We won for the simple, unchanging reason that our cause was (and remains) true and just. The opponents of trans people have none of that.

They can't understand our history or empathize with what lights the flame of activism. Their arguments are based on fear (at best) and lies too often. What they want to achieve is fundamentally unjust. For those reasons, they should not—must not—succeed. Truth and justice brought us our rights, and so long as trans people never let go of those principles, the bad guys will not succeed.

Christine Burns, MBE

THE PRESENT

This brings us neatly to the present day. Without knowing where we've been as a community, we can't know where we're going. I think it's hugely important to learn about the struggles of trans and gender-nonconforming people from history to appreciate that, even though it's **REALLY HARD** to be trans now, it was **REALLY, REALLY HARD** to be trans when there wasn't even a word to describe yourself as such.

I do think it's important that we have a label to define ourselves by, because we are a small group of people who don't have as many human rights as others. We *need* a word to describe ourselves so we can continue to fight for rights for our little group.

Moreover, I find learning about trans people from the past deeply interesting, because it makes me feel like I'm part of something much bigger than me. No two trans people are the same, and we've all walked very different paths, but we can all share stories from history and seek to unearth new ones.

Learn these stories. When transphobic people accuse you of being "trendy" or act like being trans is something new, be ready to open the library. Reading is what? Fundamental.

The bottom line is this:

TRANSGENDER
HALL OF FAME
SHANE ORTEGA

USA · THE MILITARY MILESTONE

"I think it's important to confront who you are and where you come from, because it might help you through the world. It's helped me find peace."

The former serviceman—perhaps the first to be openly trans within the U.S. armed forces—is now an LGBTQ+ advocate and a two-spirit person. This means he serves a specific ceremonial role within his Native American community that's different from our Western notion of a transgender man.

4

BEYOND THE BINARY

I am genderqueer, and to me, that means that I feel like a boy some days and like a girl some days and a mixture of both most days! You could also describe my gender as "multigender." Sometimes it's hard to explain my gender to people, because they are used to thinking of everyone as either boys or girls, but there are many of us that are neither or both.

In Indian mythology, there are loads of gods, goddesses, and otherworldly beings that are depicted as trans, and they transform from one gender to another and back over time. That is kind of how I feel on a daily basis.

Krishna Istha, performance artist

For me, it was all very simple. I was told I was a boy (slime, snails, puppy-dog tails) but knew very clearly that I was a girl (sugar, spice, all things nice). My transition was a fairly straightforward process of moving from the former to the latter.

My personal journey, no doubt, has benefitted from being very binary. I readily accepted society's very narrow definition of what a woman should look and sound like because, fortuitously, I feel comfortable enough within those parameters. Of course, like anyone, I am susceptible to damaging messages both in real life and in the media about what women should look like and how women should behave. Like all feminists, I feel women should be able to look and act however they like as long as they're not doing any harm.

Still, I feel happy in the knowledge that I'm a woman and grateful that the world (for the most part) treats me as such.

For some, it's not so simple. When, as a wee child, I looked at the very arbitrary way the Western world has been divided into two genders, I instinctively knew which camp I belonged in. But what if I hadn't? When some people regard boys and girls, men and women, they feel unable or unwilling to categorize themselves as *either*. It's no more a "choice" for them than it is for a cis or a trans person—it's just that they *aren't* boys or girls. This chapter explores those people for whom labels such as *male*, *female*, *boy*, *girl*, *man*, and *woman* don't quite cut the mustard.

HISTORICAL CONTEXT

As we learned in the last chapter, throughout history, there are a gazillion examples of people who defied the usual gender roles. We can't ask them precisely how they identified, because now they are dust, and it's quite hard to get a straight (or, indeed, gay) answer out of that.

That said, it's very clear that going all the way back to ancient times, there have been people changing their gender from the one they were assigned at birth. Again:

WE HAVE ALWAYS BEEN HERE.

THIRD/FOURTH/FIFTH GENDER

All across history and all around the globe, there are lots of records that show that ancient civilizations recognized more than two genders. In some of the earliest stories **EVER** written, literally carved in stone, the Sumerians wrote about a type of person who was neither a man or a woman.

That's from the **SECOND MILLENNIUM BCE**, and yet Piers Morgan thinks it's all very new and trendy.

If you know your history, it won't come as a surprise to learn that traditional Western notions of binary gender and sexuality were spread by dominance and invasion by European oppressors. However, some cultures persisted and continue to recognize genders beyond simply male or female. On the following pages is a table of some cultures that recognize (sometimes legally, sometimes culturally) genders beyond the binary.

GENDER	ORIGIN	LEGALLY RECOGNIZED?	DESCRIPTION
Chibados	Angola, Africa	No	Shamans in the Ndongo kingdom
Ashtime	Southern Ethiopia, Africa	No	Belonging to the small Maale culture
Mashoga	Kenya, Africa	No	Found in Swahili-speaking areas, especially Mombasa

GENDER	ORIGIN	LEGALLY RECOGNIZED?	DESCRIPTION
Mangaiko	Democratic Republic of Congo, Africa	No	From the Mbo people
Palao'ana	Micronesia, Oceania	No	Found in the Northern Mariana Islands including Guam
Fa'afafine	Samoa, Oceania	No	A recognized third gender and integral part of Samoan culture
Fakaleiti	Tonga, Oceania	No	Assigned male at birth but adopt feminine traits
Māhū or māhūwahine	Hawaii, North America	No	Treated with great respect in Hawaiian culture
Whakawahine	New Zealand, Oceania	No	Māori people have a similar concept to the above traditions found across Polynesia.
Sworn virgins	Albania and Macedonia, Europe	No	Assigned female at birth, the sworn virgins take a vow of chastity and live as men.
Muxe	Southern Mexico, Central America	No	A recognized third gender in Zapotec communities
Khanith	Oman, Arabian Peninsula	No	Assigned male at birth but fulfills traditionally female roles

GENDER	ORIGIN	LEGALLY RECOGNIZED?	DESCRIPTION
Two-spirit	North America	No	Native American term first used in 1990 to differentiate between two-spirit people, who perform a ceremonial role, and LGBTQ+ Native Americans
Hijra	India and Pakistan, South Asia	Yes	A collective term that can encapsulate intersex people, trans people, and "eunuchs." They are a legally recognized third gender not regarded as either men or women.
Kathoey	Thailand, Asia	Yes	Although many kathoeys identify as women, they are commonly regarded as a third gender and do not possess the same legal rights as cis women.

NONBINARY IDENTITIES

Increasingly, Western cultures are also recognizing that binary notions of gender don't suit everyone and are expanding legal definitions to include people who don't identify as male or female.

COUNTRIES THAT ALLOW PEOPLE TO SELF-IDENTIFY AS NONBINARY:

- Austria
- Some states in the United States
- Nepal
- (Most of) Australia
- Iceland
- New Zealand
- Canada
- Uruguay

In some places, legally, people can only be defined this way if they are intersex, which we'll discuss later. On June 30, 2021, the U.S. State Department announced that they had begun an effort to add a third gender marker on U.S. passports. In 2017, Canada introduced a gender neutral "X" on passports.

In the places listed above, people are allowed to—usually without the intervention of a medical professional—apply for ID and documentation that features an X or a blank space instead of an M or F. Simple, right? Apparently not.

KNOWING THE UNKNOWABLE

For me—a girl who always knew she was a girl—it's not much of a stretch to imagine there are people in the world who *do not* have that super strong sense of a gender. I often question if it's a bit like when I see people getting **REALLY EXCITED** about sports. I do not have that at all. There is an absence, a big fat empty nothing.

I sometimes wonder if that's what it's like to feel nonbinary or genderqueer—if there is simply an absence in the spot where I keep the *certainty* about my gender.

But why on earth would you take it from me? I'm the

most binary person I know. Therefore, I think it's very important that I hand the mic to people who know what they're talking about.

JAMIE'S STORY

Jamie Windust is something of a nonbinary legend. The British activist, model, and magazine editor spearheaded a campaign to get legal recognition for people who identify as nonbinary.

I identify as nonbinary. I got to this label because I have never felt comfortable identifying as male. At puberty, I noticed a lot more that it jarred with me. But at that time, I only knew the binary, so I wondered if I identified as female, but that didn't fit either. My education on trans issues was fairly limited. I knew I didn't want surgery or anything like that.

I spent a long time not knowing how I identified but knowing I wasn't male. I came across nonbinary issues in my first few weeks at university. It was the time of "The Transgender Tipping Point,"* and I learned about it through social media, which is disgustingly millennial. I'd never heard of nonbinary identities, but once I read it,

---

* A famous issue of *Time* magazine that featured actress Laverne Cox (see page 127).

I thought, *That's perfect*, and I found solace in that. It was only later I had to think about the logistics of living as a nonbinary person. It wasn't very euphoric, but it was a wonderful online moment.

At that time, I was still very aware that I'd been conditioned to exist as male, and I had a lot of hang-ups about the way I presented. What "looks male"? How could I push that further? I wondered how I could break down those barriers and exist day-to-day as I wanted. I could be super femme or more masculine! To me, it was navigating the spaces I existed in before—universities, work, family—but in a different way. When people transition in a binary sense, it's like they're reinvented as a new person: you go away as one thing and come back, in some way, as another person. But for me, there were no physical differences, so people struggled to understand.

TRAVIS'S STORY

Travis Alabanza is an acclaimed performance artist, whose smash-hit show *Burgerz* detailed their experience of transphobic hate.

I wish I could tell myself back then and now and in the future that things are allowed to be complicated, that your gender does not have to be simple or understood to be valid. That feeling understood is a nice feeling, yet that alone will not hold you. I never declared my transness in order to fit somewhere. I'm okay with not fitting. I know that our gender and history behind it is so much more complicated than language can encompass. We have names like *man* and *woman* and *nonbinary* because it helps us place an untouchable thing into something we can hold, but I also relax into knowing that maybe my gender is something that cannot be held or touched, that is not real and is also the realest weight I know. When the material aspects of this whole thing get to me, like the dysphoria, the stares, the harassment, the hiding, or the not knowing what to wear— sometimes holding on to how complicated and complex you are is what grounds me.

GET INTO INTERSEX

Legal issues surrounding nonbinary people are sometimes complicated by laws that state that a person can only be legally identified as such if they are what we now call **INTERSEX**.

Remember the five things that make up a person's sex?

- Gonads
- Sex chromosomes
- Sex hormones
- Internal genitalia
- External genitalia

Sometimes, a person might be born with some form of variation to one or more of these characteristics. Planned Parenthood says, "Intersex is a general term used for a variety of situations in which a person in born with reproductive or sexual anatomy that doesn't fit the boxes of 'female' or 'male.'"[*]

This variance may take many, many forms, including chromosome-level conditions such as Turner syndrome or Klinefelter syndrome, hormonal disorders like androgen insensitivity syndrome, or physical variations to the genitals (innie or outie). We don't know for certain how many people are (Lady Gaga moment) "born this way." Some U.S. research estimates about 0.05 percent of births,[†] while others believe that if we factor in more subtle variations, it's more like 1.7 percent of births,[‡] which would make it as common as having red hair.

To return to Lady Gaga for a moment, *all* LGBTQ+ people are "born this way," but some people question why we so often include conversations about intersex people alongside those about trans and nonbinary rights. Sometimes,

---

[*] "What's Intersex?" Planned Parenthood, accessed November 1, 2021, https://www.planned-parenthood.org/learn/gender-identity/sex-gender-identity/whats-intersex.

[†] "How Common Is Intersex?," Intersex Society of North America, accessed September 17, 2021, https://isna.org/faq/frequency/.

[‡] "Intersex Awareness," UN Free and Equal, accessed September 17, 2021, https://www.unfe.org/intersex-awareness/.

people raising those concerns are simply being transphobic and imply that while being intersex is a birth abnormality, being transgender is a zany whim. Other times, they are questioning whether "being intersex" is an *identity* in the same way that being LGBTQ+ is.

Well, buckle in for some T. For one thing, many intersex people do identify as such, and there is a global community with support groups and organizations. Less formally but vitally, intersex people are often assigned a gender at birth despite their variations or ambiguities. Some intersex babies are even subjected to "corrective" surgeries—which of course they cannot consent to. Therefore, the likelihood of them later transitioning once they have a better sense of their gender identity and expression or identifying as nonbinary is that much higher.

Of course, some intersex people will be gay, lesbian, or bi too. Finally, intersex people—as we'll discover shortly—face a lot of the same transphobic bullshit whether they're trans or not, so it's very, very important to include intersex people in conversations about LGBTQ+ people and also in this book.

NOTABLE INTERSEX PEOPLE

- **TONY BRIFFA:** This Australian politician is thought

to be the first intersex person to hold public office and was among the first to possess a birth certificate with a blank space for gender.

- **LADY COLIN CAMPBELL:** This author and socialite appeared on *I'm a Celebrity...Get Me Out of Here!* in 2015.

- **CAROLINE COSSEY:** As "Tula," she appeared in the Bond film *For Your Eyes Only* in 1981.

- **HANNE GABY ODIELE:** This supermodel spoke out against performing surgeries on intersex infants in 2017.

- **PIDGEON PAGONIS:** This writer and activist appeared in an episode of *Transparent* in 2016.

The cases of two athletes—Dutee Chand and Caster Semenya—have highlighted the ignorance and discrimination intersex people can face. Neither woman has publicly spoken about being intersex, although there has been fevered speculation about both athletes that I won't add to here. Needless to say, years of being accused of cheating, various panels and appeals, countless column inches about alleged "hormonal advantages," and attempts to force them to take hormone suppressants have taken a toll. Semenya says the ongoing attempts to ban her from competition have left her "destroyed—mentally and physically."

We are talking about human rights. We are talking about people being freed. People living their lives for who they are. It's wrong to judge people. It's wrong to discriminate [against] people and also to divide people.

We are all human. It doesn't matter what differences we have in our bodies. At the end of the day, sport unites people and it speaks to the youth in a language they understand.

Why do you have to drug someone? So you want them to fit in...

It's very simple...when you introduced sports, you never said people with differences cannot run with other people. You do not say we categorize men because they have got long legs, they have got long arms. They have those long strides. Others are short. You don't categorize them like that. You categorize them as women and men.

Caster Semenya (interviewed by Ade Adedoyin for BBC Sport in 2019)

JOSEPH'S STORY

Makeup artist and creative director Joseph "JoJo" Harwood has accumulated over forty million views on YouTube. After a turbulent adolescence, Joseph discovered they were, after all, intersex—although that's not necessarily how they identify.

I don't really know where I fit anymore with these terms. I have never been as fussed about labels as I am about humanization—I don't mind what you call me as long as you say it with a smile. I guess I'm nonbinary because I play with my gender expression consciously.

Through puberty, I grew breasts and didn't develop brow ridging or a prominent Adam's apple. I went to the doctor with a list of symptoms ranging from passing out, memory loss, and body dysphoria to major mood swings, which is identical to what any cis female would go through in menopause, and yet was told that nothing was wrong. I should have been given a proper look-over as a toddler when I came home from school saying I was a girl, but it never happened because the doctors were working from an antiquated position of understanding.

I had a horrendous experience of puberty. It really was a nightmare that I had to trial and error a solution with. I don't think that there's any kind of support for people unless it's a specific type of transition. I've wanted to remove my breast tissues and female characteristics to a point that I can be something more in the middle, angelic. I have been on different combinations of HRT and transitioned to find autonomy in my body. That's where I've been and my experience.

As I've progressed through my transition, cheerfully complying with white Western norms of what a woman should look like, I've started to notice that **CONFORMING** gets you far. That's why, to me, anyone defying the rigid gender norms—however you identify—is an absolute boss.

Don't get me wrong. *Anyone* challenging the gender they were assigned at birth is astonishingly brave, but it takes real courage to live as a nonbinary person in our very binary world.

With fewer legal protections that even transgender people, nonbinary people need all our support, respect, and love.

TRANSGENDER HALL OF FAME

HANNE GABY ODIELE

BELGIUM · THE INTERSEX ICON

"Intersex is just a part of who I am, like the color of my hair. It doesn't define who I am. I'm intersex and I'm proud."

It may not define her, but Odiele's admission in 2017 shone a much-needed light on what it means to be intersex. She has since spoken out against forcing gender-confirming surgeries on infants and toddlers while continuing her career as a top-flight fashion model.

5

Y THO?

Let's be very clear on one thing: being transgender is not in any way a sickness, illness, disease, or affliction. In fact, in 2018, the World Health Organization declassified "gender incongruence" as a mental illness. In short, trans or nonbinary identities are not in themselves mental illnesses, although we know that people in both groups are much more likely to suffer from other mental health problems, are more likely to become HIV positive, and are more likely to experience sexual violence (not because being trans is terrible but because the world around us treats us terribly).

Don't forget that the WHO classified homosexuality as a mental illness up until 1992. These medical classifications are problematic, because if we treat someone's identity as a sickness, it suggests there is a cure. The sheer notion that LGBTQ+ people can be "cured" is deadly. In the United States, the American Medical Association and GLMA:

Health Professionals Advancing LGBTQ Equality oppose the use of reparative or conversion therapy for sexual orientation or gender identity.

It's interesting, though, to occasionally ponder *what made me this way?* I have no doubt in my mind that as soon as I plopped out of my mum, this was pretty much my destiny: outwardly male but very much a girl on the inside. From birth. Given how hard my parents, school, and society worked to keep me on the straight and cis-narrow, I'm assuming there was something biological at my core that has made me feel so strongly about my gender.

Now, before we examine some of the *theories* about transgender people—and they are just that—I always say that no straight or cisgender person has ever needed to do the emotional (not to mention scientific) labor on this. Being trans is phenomenally hard work, because society suddenly expects you to be an expert on:

- General studies
- Endocrinology
- Neuropsychology
- Feminism
- Criminal law
- Genealogy

And that's just for starters. Come on, guys! I just wanna watch *Love Island* and cuddle my dog! I'm not an expert on any of those things, and nor do you have to be. No one

expects that of straight or cisgender people, and LGBTQ+ people do not owe *anyone* an explanation as to why we're allowed to take up space on the planet.

That said, various scientists have attempted to explain our 0.6 percent of the population. When something keeps recurring, I suppose it'd be weird if they didn't study us. That's what scientists do, after all. Over the years, they have come up with various competing theories that may offer some answers as to why we're (Lady Gaga starts again) "born this way." To be honest, a lot of this stuff is **SUPER SCIENCE-Y** and **SUPER COMPLICATED.**

I hereby grant you a pass to skip to the next chapter, but it is fairly interesting stuff if you're up for some **THEORIES.**

BRAIN DEVELOPMENT

Once upon a time, it was thought that gender identity was entirely a social construct, with our identity solidifying when we're between one and four years old.* More recently, the thinking is that gender identity is hardwired in our

---

* Ai-Min Bao and Dick F. Swaab, "Sexual Differentiation of the Human Brain: Relation to Gender Identity, Sexual Orientation, and Neuropsychiatric Disorders," *Frontiers in Neuroendocrinology* 32, no. 2 (April 2011): 214–26, https://doi.org/10.1016/j.yfrne.2011.02.007; Louis J. G. Gooren, "Hormone Treatment of the Adult Transsexual Patient," *Hormone Research* 64, Suppl. 2 (2005): 31–36, https://doi.org/10.1159/000087751.

brains from birth, although the way we're socialized can potentially override this programming.

This means that there's a fascinating nature/nurture conversation to be had. We already know that gender is a social construct, but do those "rules" about gender that we hold so dear come from something programmed within us? It's interesting, philosophically, but I wouldn't dwell on it too much.

I remember my A level biology class being **SHOOK** when our teacher explained that a clitoris is, in fact, an undeveloped penis. A quick online search will throw up the fact that all babies start out female in the womb, and it's only later that they become male, and this is at least *somewhat* true. More accurately, we start out with the same *genderless* embryonic structure for about eight weeks. Yep, each one of us was once **A BLOB**, albeit a blob with XX or XY chromosomes that are supposed to provide a blueprint for our sexual development.

While we're a-brewing in someone's tummy, we're marinated in a heady soup of hormones. One of these is testosterone, and if there's enough of it, it can mold our features from something that looks female into something that looks male.*

Okay, it gets even more science-y now: testosterone production and the conversion of some testosterone to something called dihydrotestosterone between weeks six and twelve of pregnancy are critical for the initial development of external male genitalia. In the absence of these male hormones, female genitalia develop instead. Brain development, however, doesn't really take place until the latter half of pregnancy, after the genitals have developed.†

So you can probably predict the twist. Given that the hormonal impact on brain development happens at two stages, what if **SOMETHING GOES AWRY** between these two steps, leading to a mismatch between bodily sex at birth and the gender that gets wired into a brain? Boom! You have a trans baby, baby!

There is a wealth of evidence for the notion that we're all a product of hormonal cocktails in utero. Scientist types Bao, Swaab, and Gooren, often working with a multitude of different intersex people with varying conditions, point at how being exposed to too many or too few

---

* Louis J. G. Gooren, "The Biology of Human Psychosexual Differentiation," *Hormones and Behavior* 50, no. 4 (November 2006): 589–601, https://doi.org/10.1016/j.yhbeh.2006.06.011.
† Bao and Swaab, "Sexual Differentiation."

testosterone-based chemicals in the womb are likely to create this disparity—or dysphoria—between body and mind.

I suppose what they're suggesting is that *all* transgender people are on an intersex spectrum if you like. In some of us, it affected our bodies and, in others, only our brain development.

FAMILY STUDIES

Does our position in the running order of our siblings affect our likelihood of being trans, or are we actually inheriting the trait? Family studies are usually trying to root out evidence of genes. So could there be a transgender gene?

- Straight trans women are more likely to be the younger or youngest children in families with more brothers than sisters.[‡]
- Twin studies have shown a hereditary component for gender dysphoria.[§]
- One study of gender dysphoria in 314 twins found a heritable trait, implying a strong genetic trait.

---

‡ Bao and Swaab, "Sexual Differentiation."
§ Bao and Swaab, "Sexual Differentiation."

Basically, if one twin was trans, there was a higher likelihood that their sibling would be too.*

- In some very rare cases, two or more trans people have been born into a single family generation,† and in some cases, trans kids have a trans parent.‡

All these studies therefore suggest there may be a trans gene somewhere in there. *strokes chin*

BRAIN STRUCTURE

As you'd expect, when studying trans people, many scientists have started with our brains. Some of them have found there are very, *very* subtle differences up in our skulls. I mean, these differences are so tiny, you can't see them on an X-ray, nor even an MRI, without specifically looking for them. If there really was a "trans brain," we'd be able to

---

* Frederick L. Coolidge, Linda L. Thede, and Susan E. Young, "The Heritability of Gender Identity Disorder in a Child and Adolescent Twin Sample," *Behavior Genetics* 32, no. 4 (July 2002): 251–57, https://doi.org/10.1023/a:1019724712983.

† R. Green, "Family Cooccurrence of 'Gender Dysphoria': Ten Sibling or Parent-Child Pairs," *Archives of Sexual Behavior* 29, no. 5 (October 2000): 499–507, https://doi.org/10.1023/a:1001947920872; Robert F. Sabalis et al., "The Three Sisters: Transsexual Male Siblings," *American Journal of Psychiatry* 131, no. 8 (August 1974): 907–9, https://doi.org/10.1176/ajp.131.8.907; Majid Sadeghi and Ali Fakhrai, "Transsexualism in Female Monozygotic Twins: A Case Report," *Australian & New Zealand Journal of Psychiatry* 34, no. 5 (October 2000): 862–64, https://doi.org/10.1080/j.1440-1614.2000.00804.x.

‡ Green, "Family Cooccurrence."

"diagnose" it super young and just let trans people get on with their lives without them continually having to plead for acceptance.

The thing with brain studies is that we all have slightly different brains anyway, regardless of gender, so the studies aren't exactly airtight. Truly, we are all special snowflakes when it comes to brains.

Keeping all that in mind, let us look at the evidence.

- Cis men have about twice the volume and twice the number of neurons as cis women in two specific regions of the brain.[§] An early study of brains in dead bodies found that trans women have roughly the same numbers of neurons in these areas as cis women.[¶] The same result was observed in living trans patients too.[**]

- One trans man who was tested was found to have the same number of neurons as a cisgender man.[††] Obviously, this result isn't representative.

---

§ Bao and Swaab, "Sexual Differentiation"; Frank P. M. Kruijver et al., "Male-to-Female Transsexuals Have Female Neuron Numbers in a Limbic Nucleus," *Journal of Clinical Endocrinology & Metabolism* 85, no. 5 (May 2000): 2034–41, https://doi.org/10.1210/jcem.85.5.6564.

¶ Jiang-Ning Zhou et al., "A Sex Difference in the Human Brain and Its Relation to Transsexuality," *Nature* 378, no. 6552 (November 1995): 68–70.

** Bao and Swaab, "Sexual Differentiation"; Kruijver et al., "Male-to-Female Transsexuals."

†† Bao and Swaab, "Sexual Differentiation"; Kruijver et al., "Male-to-Female Transsexuals."

- MRI data from twenty-four trans women who had not received hormone treatment revealed that while their overall gray matter appeared similar to that of cis men, they possessed a significantly larger amount of gray matter in one particular part of the brain. In fact, the trans women's brains were much closer to those seen in cis women subjects. In short, while the brains of the trans women resembled cis male brains in terms of gray matter, in one specific region, their brains appeared to be "feminized."[*]

- A study using imaging technology of the brains of eighteen trans men (who weren't on hormone therapy), twenty-four cis men, and nineteen cis women showed that the white-matter structure of trans men was much closer to that of cis men than that of cis women.[†]

- A follow-up study found that after the trans men had received hormone treatment, significant changes occurred in their brains, making them appear even

---

[*]   Eileen Luders et al., "Regional Gray Matter Variation in Male-to-Female Transsexualism," *NeuroImage* 46, no. 4 (July 2009): 904–7, https://doi.org/10.1016/j.neuroimage.2009.03.048.

[†]   Giuseppina Rametti et al., "White Matter Microstructure in Female-to-Male Transsexuals before Cross-Sex Hormonal Treatment: A Diffusion Tensor Imaging Study," *Journal of Psychiatric Research* 45, no. 2 (February 2011): 199–204, https://doi.org/10.1016/j.jpsychires.2010.05.006.

more masculinized in certain regions that are associated with cis men.[‡]

- An MRI study of trans women and men examined the shape of something called the corpus callosum in the brain and compared this shape with that observed in cis men and women. The results demonstrated that not only could the sex of the patient be determined with 74 percent accuracy from the MRI picture, but the shapes of the trans patients' brains strongly reflected their gender, not their biological sex.[§]

- A more recent study examined cortical thickness (which I think sounds vaguely sexy) in the brain between cis and trans people who had not received hormone treatment. Using MRI scans, researchers found that the trans women had more cortical thickness than the cis males. The trans men showed evidence of masculinization of their gray matter.[¶]

[‡] Giuseppina Rametti et al., "Effects of Androgenization on the White Matter Microstructure of Female-to-Male Transsexuals: A Diffusion Tensor Imaging Study," *Psychoneuroendocrinology* 37, no. 8 (August 2012): 1261–9, https://doi.org/10.1016/j.psyneuen.2011.12.019.

[§] Y. Yokota, Y. Kawamura, and Y. Kameya, "Callosal Shapes at the Midsagittal Plane: MRI Differences of Normal Males, Normal Females, and GID," *2005 IEEE Engineering in Medicine and Biology 27th Annual Conference*, (2005): 3055–58.

[¶] Leire Zubiaurre-Elorza et al., "Cortical Thickness in Untreated Transsexuals," *Cerebral Cortex* 23, no. 12 (December 2013): 2855–62, https://doi.org/10.1093/cercor/bhs267.

WHAT DOES THIS ALL MEAN?

So what can we take away from all this excellent science?

Well, for one thing, every single study above has been challenged on the grounds of small sample size. This is not surprising. After all, trans people make up such a tiny percentage of the population. Other researchers were unable to observe the differences noted by the listed scientists.

You know what?

I think it's all pointless.

For one thing, this is what we call the "pathologizing" of trans lives. The studies treat us as patients when we're actually people. To be trans isn't to be sick or broken. Some of us may choose a path that involves medical treatment, but not all.

The fact is—regardless of those interesting, chin-stroking theories—trans people are people. Online trolls love to say they're "pro science" when they call trans people freaks, so it doesn't hurt to know that science is on our side. However, if you are pleading with some grim-faced transphobe about your cortical thickness, I think you're dealing with an asshole who doesn't deserve your time, frankly.

It should be enough for you to say, "I am a woman," "I am a man," or "I am nonbinary."

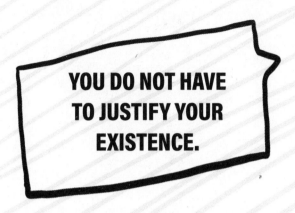

YOU DO NOT HAVE TO JUSTIFY YOUR EXISTENCE.

As we established in the last chapter, trans people have been around forever. We are real, and we are valid. We don't need a reason. We are.

TRANSGENDER HALL OF FAME

CHAZ BONO

USA · THE TRANSMASCULINE TRAILBLAZER

"I wanted to show America a different kind of man. If there was someone like me when I was growing up, my whole life would have been different."

As the son of pop star Cher, Chaz was used to being in the public eye, but he moved trans awareness forward light-years when he came out in 2009. He has since appeared on *Dancing with the Stars*, *RuPaul's Drag Race*, and *American Horror Story*.

PART TWO

TRANS LIFE

6

COMING OUT

Since *This Book Is Gay* came out in 2014, I'd say a good 50 percent of the fan mail I get is from young LGBTQ+ people asking for advice about coming out to their friends and family. Frustratingly, I always reply that I'm in no position to give cast-iron advice, because the sad fact is there is no easy way to do it and absolutely no way of predicting the response. After all, I don't know your exact circumstances. Like Galadriel in *Lord of the Rings*, I do not trust myself with that power.

In life, as with clothing, one size does not fit all. That said, there are absolutely some fairly solid *guidance* notes I can offer, fully understanding that things never go quite according to plan anyway.

I've come out twice (I mean, it's **SO FUN**), and I can assure you, it will feel like the world is going to end, but I can also assure you that the world won't end. That's the most important thing to consider. Every fab LGBTQ+ role model you have has done it all before and lived to tell the tale. It's like going to the dentist: it may well be uncomfortable, even painful, but you'll probably be glad you went there in the end.

WHY BOTHER?

This is a really valid question. Another very common sort of email I get—especially if I'm on television—comes from people who feel they would like to transition (whatever form that may take) but, for a litany of reasons, feel they cannot. Always remember these key points:

- No one should ever feel pressured to come out or make grand statements about their gender and/or sexuality.
- No one should feel they only have one "go" at coming out. You can redefine your gender or sexuality as many times as you see fit.

But there are oodles of benefits to coming out. Again, I'd only ever speak for myself, but it did feel—until I was thirty years old—that I was living half my life, occupying half my existence. I knew who I was, but I was only living as Juno in my skull. By coming out, I was able to exist to my fullest potential.

It's no fun living with shame and secrets. I think living out loud as gay, lesbian, bi, trans, or nonbinary is very freeing. Personally, I didn't like keeping secrets about myself from my friends and family. Once I came out, I found that I felt *more* loved, because I knew my nearest and dearest loved all of me from head to, well, T.

I don't get a commission every time someone new comes out, so I'm not here to convince or recruit anyone to do anything. What I will say is that while living my truth as a trans woman has been difficult at times, **NEVER ONCE** have I regretted coming out—to other people or myself.

YOU CAME OUT TO YOURSELF?

Yes, that does sound a bit odd, but before you do the whole tearful confession bit, the first—and most difficult—admission is the one you make to yourself.

Every ad, TV show, billboard, movie, and newspaper has subliminally told you that being LGBTQ+ is less than normal, a suboptimum outcome. If being cis and straight has always been presented to you as the best possible situation, you can see why it could be so hard to admit to yourself that you are potentially something other than cis or straight. That's why we can't say it enough: there is **NOTHING AT ALL** wrong with being LGBTQ+. It's not that something went awry; it's just how it is. Just as we need to equally celebrate every skin color and body type as "normal," we must also admit—as a society—that being LGBTQ+ is normal for LGBTQ+ people. That is who and what we are. You are perfectly you.

Still, as long as it's assumed that every last bébé plopped onto this planet is both cis and straight, a whole bunch of us will (a) have to come to the realization that we're not and (b) go through an enormous practical and emotional hardship to put people right.

There is a closet. It was built for us by straight and cis people, who also constructed a society that suited them. While that is in place, annoyingly, we do have to make a choice about whether to step out of it. Again, this is an emotional labor that straight and cis people will never really understand. And that is important to bear in mind if the people you're about to come out to are those things.

HOW TO COME OUT

I really can't stress this enough—there is no "correct" way to do this. So the following is a very general list of ideas that you may wish to ponder before you take the plunge.

1. DON'T GET IT TWISTED

The only drawback to coming out is that you are somewhat labeling yourself, and once labeled, it can be hard to take back. Personally, I'm fine with you having as many different labels as you want, but in order to avoid people challenging or questioning your identity, it might be wise to consider the following points ahead of the big day:

- How do you feel?
- How long have you felt this way?
- What do you want to change in your life, if anything?
- Do you have any particular goals, like different pronouns, a different name, etc.?

Getting those points straight (ha!) in your head will help you remain focused despite your nerves and anxiety about the task ahead.

2. DECIDE WHO YOU'RE TELLING

It makes sense to tell someone you absolutely trust first. This could be a parent, caregiver, friend, teacher, or doctor. Finding a trusted buddy is also a really good way to iron out the complicated worries in your head. Your gender and identity are very complicated. Why should you have to figure it out all by yourself?

It's totally fine to say to your confidant, "**I'VE BEEN DOING A LOT OF THINKING ABOUT MY GENDER RECENTLY.**" You don't have to have all the answers one hundred percent ready. Uncertainty and confusion get a bad rep, but they are perfectly natural parts of life. God, imagine claiming to be wholly certain all the time. Only psychopaths and politicians do that.

Personally, I went down the therapy route (because privilege) and spent literally a year doing a lot of thinking about my gender. A whole year! That's a lot of thinking. But I've been known to spend *months* dwelling on my next haircut, and that's just on my head. Your gender identity isn't something you want to rush.

However, if you do want to affect changes in your life (your pronouns or your name or your physical appearance), you will have to make some sort of statement eventually. Exhausting, but necessary.

3. PICK YOUR MOMENT

As your nana's casket makes its way down the church aisle is not the optimum moment to announce you want people to use they/them pronouns. Indeed, there are practical considerations to take into account when planning to come out.

I mean, it doesn't need to be a big *Greatest Showman* moment with elephants and acrobats. It could be a very gradual, organic process of subtly adapting your clothes, hair, or makeup (your gender expression) until such a time that people start to ask if you'd like them to use a different name or pronoun. That does sometimes happen—especially with peers.

However, a lot of the stress seems to stem from family members. Some parents or caregivers are amazingly supportive and, as above, initiate the difficult conversations. But for some, this is all going to come as a big old surprise. It's kinder, therefore, to come out considerately.

Sure, sometimes best-laid plans go to hell and you might well end up screaming **"I'M TRANS, YOU MORONS!"** at your parents during a heated row. While I believe any argument is fixable, it's better to plan ahead and set the scene a little.

WHERE?

I think a private place is best, somewhere quiet where you can have a proper conversation. Home is fine, but perhaps

plan to go out later so you can give them some space to process what you've told them.

WHEN?

There's no ideal time to drop home truths, but trying to cram it into the commercial break of *The Great British Baking Show* might not be the best idea. It's likely to be a long conversation, so give it some time.

WHO?

Specifically, do you tackle a whole bunch of people at once or do a series of one-to-one conversations? There are pros and cons to both, but remember you can ask one person how they think another is likely to react or ask for their help. For instance, could a trusted sibling help you come out to your parents? Could your mum help you tell your dad?

HOW?

I always think a face-to-face conversation is best wherever possible, although my therapist advised me to write a letter to my father. I lived many miles away, and the therapist said a letter or email is a solid way to say everything you want to say in a rational way—and you have the power to get a friend to read a draft. The other advantage is that the other party has a chance to think about their response in a calm way too. The downside of a letter or email is that they're quite impersonal, *and* it's very hard to convey tone in the written word. A wrong word and you can accidentally sound angry, for example.

4. CHOOSE YOUR WORDS

I'm not going to give you a script. Only you know the people you trust to know the real you. What follows is more like guidance.

"CAN WE TALK?"

This lets you establish if now is a good time for the person you want to tell. Yes, you're going through some things, but they might be too. People only have so much emotional capacity. Try to find a time that's good for everyone. Of course, if a person is repeatedly avoiding conversations with you, you may have to be more forceful and say it can't wait.

"I'VE BEEN THINKING A LOT ABOUT MY GENDER."

This gives them *some* sort of warning of what's about to come.

"SINCE I WAS..."

Give them some sense of a timeline. This way, they're less likely to use the dreaded "It's just a phase."

"THIS IS WHAT'S GOING TO HAPPEN."

Thanks to some very patchy media reporting, the people you're coming out to are likely to have *wildly* inaccurate notions of what being trans or nonbinary is all about. The most persistent myth, of course, is that all trans people opt for surgery or that trans youth have *any* surgery. It may be helpful to inform the people you love about what *does* happen. The technical side of transition will be covered in chapter 9, but this would also be where to tell them what your end goals are, if you know them. Do you want to use different pronouns? Choose a different name? Medically transition? Once again, you absolutely don't have to have all the answers right away, but can you let them know what will change in the immediate future? It might be that, right now, you don't want to make any changes. It might be enough for you to share that you're in a period of reflection. Similarly, do you have any information you can give them? The Trevor Project, Transgender Law Center, and the ACLU all provide assistance in the United States, or you could just give them a copy of this book!

"TAKE SOME TIME TO PROCESS THIS."

You can't info dump on your nearest and dearest and expect them not to have any opinions whatsoever. Nor can you expect them to organize an impromptu parade in your honor. That *might* happen. Most people, I found, were wonderfully supportive.*

The piece of advice I give out the most is urging readers to be **PATIENT**. However long you've been mulling on your gender identity, you can bet that everyone else has been spending considerably less time thinking about it. Even if you were that stereotypical gender-nonconforming tomboy or whatever, expect there to be some surprise and shock.

When I came out, I provided my mother with some information pamphlets to read through, but she still, understandably, had a lot of questions. Expect a *lot* of questions, and be prepared to answer them. I call this period **THE SKY IS FALLING**.

For a brief time, your family life, or life in general, may go into crisis mode.

There may be tears and difficult conversations, but rest assured, this period is nearly always temporary.

---

* This is why we get to choose our friends. We instinctively seek out people we sense are inclusive and gradually distance ourselves from the weenies.

This is why I suggest planning a cooling-off period after the initial conversation. You will not badger people into being cool within half an hour. Yes, it would be lovely, but it's unlikely to happen. Time, gratefully, is a healer.

"I AM STILL ME."

This a really good one to end on. I think what people fear—especially parents—is losing a child. Some parents of trans people report bereavement-like responses to a coming out. There's this kid they love, and that kid is going to vanish. This is absolutely not the case. In fact, their child is simply evolving into their truest form. Their child is about to be *even more* their child.

Appearance-wise, you've changed a lot, obviously. But in your personality, no, I don't think you've changed much at all.

Angela Dawson, my mum

Assure people that the real you—the one on the inside—isn't going to change, except, notably, you'll be much more contented if allowed to express your gender identity in a way that makes you comfortable. Who wouldn't want you to be happy?

5. PREPARE IN CASE IT GOES WRONG

Because sometimes it does, although it's very, *very* rare. It might take *years*, but even the most ruined bridges can be rebuilt. Go into this assuming that you are loved and that your friends and family don't want to lose you. Yes, there might be gnarly moments, but you are a precious thing, and they will want to keep you in their lives.

I think it's common to underestimate people—especially our parents. I've said this all over the place—because I think it's important—but my relationship with my father is better now than it ever was pretransition. That's right: living as your authentic self can actually *improve* your relationships. Don't go into all this assuming the worst, but prepare for a bumpy ride. Life insurance, if you like.

That said, if things get really bad, know there are organizations such as the Trevor Project, Trans Lifeline, and Transgender Law Center that can provide practical support should things go wrong. More information can be found in chapter 17.

6. REMEMBER THAT COMING OUT IS A PROCESS

Here's the thing with coming out: the first time is the hardest, but you'll actually find yourself coming out so often, you'll soon forget what the fuss was about.

Again, because the world assumes everyone is straight

and cis, you'll find yourself continually repeating yourself forever. I remember, with some horror, realizing I was going to have to come out **AGAIN** when I got to college, having gone through the whole process the year before in school. That second time, it was easy. The third time, it was easier still. Since 1997, I must have come out about a million times. For now, although frequently tedious, it's part of the LGBTQ+ experience.

TRANSGENDER HALF OF FAME

LAVERNE COX

USA · THE A-LIST ACTRESS

"I think trans women, and trans people in general, show everyone that you can define what it means to be a man or woman on your own terms. A lot of what feminism is about is moving outside of roles and moving outside of expectations of who and what you're supposed to be to live a more authentic life."

In 2014, actress and activist Cox appeared on a very famous *Time* magazine cover declaring the "The Trans Tipping Point." Truly a global icon, Cox has become possibly the most recognizable voice of the trans community—if such a thing can truly ever exist. From *Vogue* and *Cosmopolitan* covers to *Orange Is the New Black*, *Charlie's Angels*, and her tireless activism, Cox introduced trans issues to people who previously thought we were a myth.

7
THE TRANS LIFE

Once you've got the whole coming out bit over and done with, what next? Like I said before, pretty much every grown-ass LGBTQ+ person has gone through a similar process and lived to tell the tale. And *lived* is the important word there—you now have the rest of your life to adjust, acclimatize, and just, well, *be*.

Dawn Summers once memorably told her sister, Buffy the Vampire Slayer, that the hardest thing to do in this world is live in it, and she was so right. After all the expectation of coming out, the last thing you want is the rest of your life to feel like an anticlimax. Luckily, after all the drama, life quickly eases into your new reality.

Eventually, the dust settles, you look around, and you're like, okay, what's next? First of all, some key terms.

GOING STEALTH

This phrase refers to trans people who, for lots of reasons, choose not to disclose their transgender status in day-to-day life. Some people prefer to "blend in" to society without openly identifying as part of a community. That's a choice some people make, and of course, we should respect that.

PASSING

This is another word we'll be using a lot. The notion of passing refers to trans people who "pass" as cisgender; in other words, they are not obviously transgender to the casual onlooker.

Passing and *going stealth* are important terms, because anyone who is in *any* way gender nonconforming is going to draw attention to themselves in public. Sadly, this is very much part and parcel of the transgender experience. I'll discuss transphobia in great depth in chapter 8, but for now, it is enough to say that the struggle is real.

Anyway, let's not get ahead of ourselves, and start with a positive. **HURRAH!** You're trans or nonbinary! Woo-hoo! Welcome to the rest of your life!

Now, unlike coming out as gay, lesbian, queer, or bisexual (or maybe you did that at the same time), people do rather expect a physical transformation once you've come out as trans or nonbinary. In fact, it can feel like a bit of pressure.

Fear not! You have the rest of your life to fully inhabit, embrace, and understand your body and style. There is no rush whatsoever. I'm inclined to say that one of the bonuses of coming out is that you're now fully free to defy **GENDER EXPECTATIONS**. You're no longer constricted by those tedious rules that say "boys can wear this" or "girls wear that." That's the dictionary definition of gender nonconforming!

It's sort of the whole point—by being you, you're being a rule breaker. Own it!

May I now present a special half-time show from our supremely talented illustrator, Soofiya!

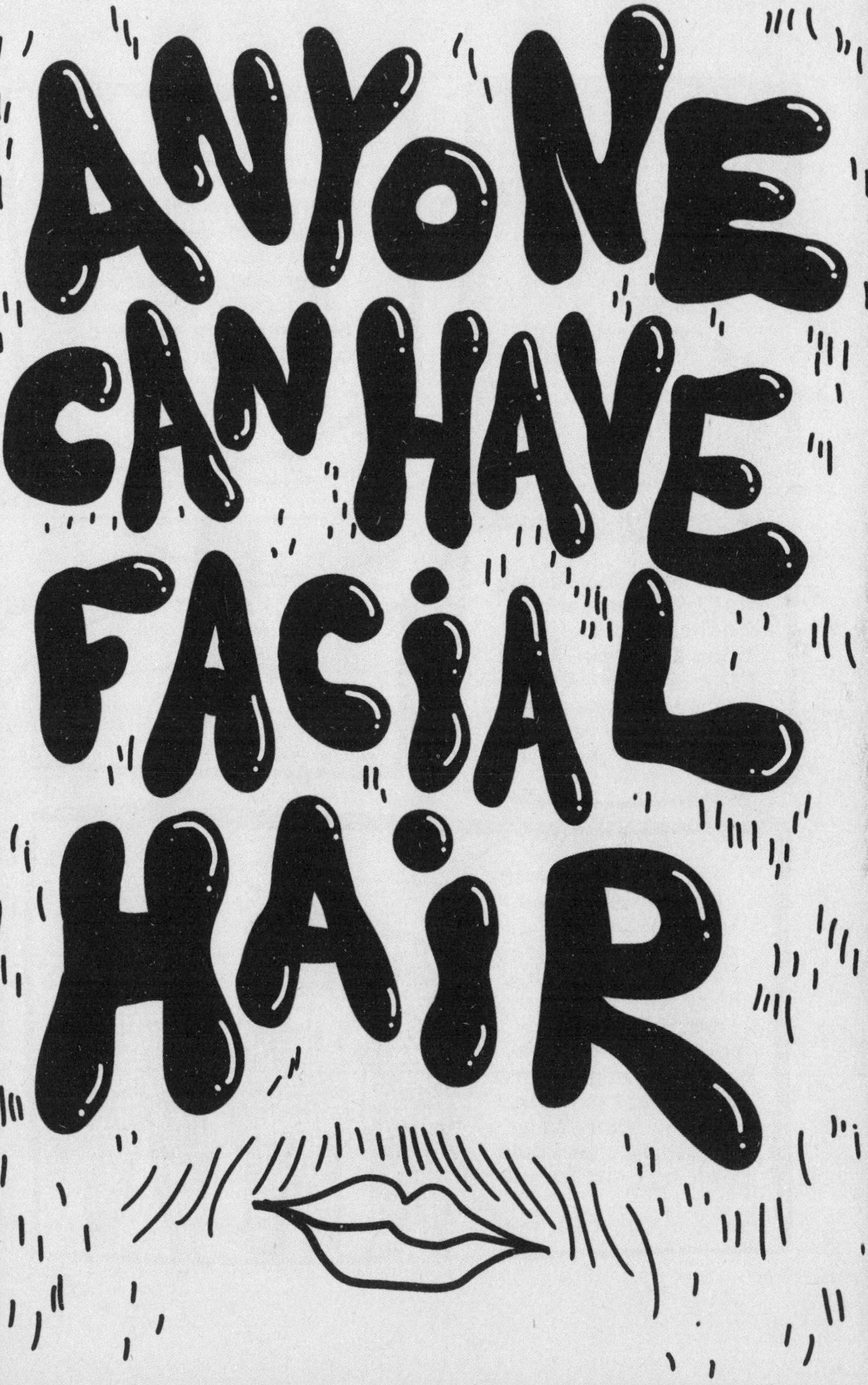
ANYONE CAN HAVE FACIAL HAIR

So let this be a reminder, on days you might need to hear it: facial hair doesn't make or break your gender. Gender isn't about how you look or don't look. It can be so much more than that. My gender-nonconforming body taught me this a long time ago.

YOU DO YOU!

I'm not saying it's *mandatory* that all gender-nonconforming people dye their hair a pastel shade, but it's certainly very popular.

That's in jest, obviously, but there's something to it. When you've spent a chunk of your life toeing the line with a set of gender norms you felt very at odds with, of course you're going to celebrate breaking free of those shackles.

In the earliest days of my transition, I felt very out of control, so I did little things that gave me a greater sense of ownership of my gender: I got my ears pierced; I dyed my hair (albeit not a pastel shade); I altered the clothes I was wearing; I started paying for laser treatment on my facial hair. Nothing hugely life altering, but I took back control.

A bit later on, I got some hair extensions and bought some very traditionally female clothes. This was around the time I legally changed my name to Juno.

HOW TO "PASS" PHYSICALLY

I am, in a way, loathe to write this section, because trans and/ or nonbinary people shouldn't have to "pass" as anything in order to make cis people feel more comfortable. The whole point of nonbinary identities is rejecting any notion of being a man or a woman!

The best way to "pass" is to be yourself and know that you are that dude!

Roshaante Anderson, model

Really and truly, why do we give a damn?

Passing is such a big deal in the trans community. Many hinge their idea of a "successful" transition on it, or [see it] as a form of validation. Others fear not passing because being more visibly trans may put their safety at risk or leave them open to harassment and discrimination.

I find the idea of passing very damaging.

The thing about passing is that you have no control over whether or not it's possible for you—it's based on other people's perspectives and their definition of gender. Yeah, hormone replacement therapy (if you decide that's a part of your journey) can help, but you can't determine how masculine or feminine it will make you, and again, how people will perceive you.

The reality is, passing means nothing if you're not happy within yourself.

I think trans people believe that passing will solve all their life problems, but take it from someone who has been passing for many years: it doesn't. You may still suffer with dysphoria (I do sometimes), and you will still have to engage in all the difficult conversations.

Transitioning is complicated, but so are human beings. Gender doesn't have to look a certain way; just like your personality is unique to you, so is your gender expression. Your focus doesn't have to be passing or proving who you are to anyone else, because no amount of acceptance from others will give you the same feeling of freedom as accepting yourself.

Kenny Ethan Jones, model and activist

That said, is it *easier* to go about town and do a bit of shopping if you don't have a load of rude little kids pointing you out? Is it *safer*? Yes, very much so. It's not so much about passing some imaginary gender exam so much as it is getting by. Yes, I had a very distinct notion of how I wanted to look, but really, all I ever wanted was to get by. It's not our fault that society can be quite hostile toward gender-nonconforming people, so I don't think we should feel bad for wanting an easier ride.

The problem with passing is that it reinforces very binary ideals of what men and women "should" look like: men should be big, tall, and muscular, while women should be petite, slender, and delicate.

Clearly, that's a load of crap on a plate. Passing is a thorny subject, and a great many trans and/or nonbinary people want no part of that gendered malarkey. But some do, and that's fine too. As I've said many times, there's no right or wrong way to be trans, and people who want to pass or go stealth are every bit as valid as those who don't. But do feel free to skip this segment if it's not your jam.

As with coming out, there isn't one universal way to pass, whether you're transmasculine (describing people who *mostly* align with masculinity, without needing to be a "man") or transfeminine (describing people who *mostly* align with femininity, without needing to be a "woman"). Nor is there an exam, although it often feels like we're all failing at some secret test. I wonder if anyone, cis or trans, really feels like they're "winning" at being a man or a woman.*

All that said, did I want to pass? **HELL YES.** Do a lot of

---

* This was the entire basis of my book *The Gender Games,* should you wish to read more.

trans people want to? Also yes. I think it comes back to bodily autonomy. Everyone should be able to look precisely how they want, even if that's a very stereotypical construct of how a man or woman "ought" to look.

With this in mind, here are just a few tips I wish some kind trans sister had taught me in the early days. A caveat: remember, I was well past puberty when I started my transition and didn't have access to puberty blockers. For younger trans people who dodged the bullet of the wrong puberty, some of these may not be relevant.

For Those Aiming for "Feminine"
MAKEUP

At the end of the day, testosterone changes faces to have more "masculine" features. These can include a heavier brow bone, larger nose, squarer jaw, and higher hairline. Luckily, we can change the proportion of a face with makeup.

Contouring is often used by drag queens to create the illusion of a feminine face by closing in the perimeter using darker makeup and highlighting the central features. I'm not going to explain how to do that here because (a) I was always crap at it, and (b) there are a gazillion YouTube tutorials that'll show you how.

Naturally, any makeup will signal to the world that you are in some way "femme" because—as depressing as it is—all makeup is coded as feminine.

I have benefitted hugely from having worked with hundreds of makeup artists on photo shoots and TV shows and learned from all of them. A lot of chain stores, including Sephora, train their staff to work with trans people, so why not go learn from the professionals? YouTube can guide you too.

FACIAL HAIR

If you've reached the age where you are growing facial hair, don't panic. Everyone—men and women, cis and trans—gets some facial hair. You can leave it (people will just have to deal with it) or have it removed in a number of ways: threading, waxing, or hair-removal creams. If you've developed a full-on beard, you may need to access laser removal if you want it gone.

Covering more mature facial hair with makeup can be tricky. As a white woman, I found it helpful to "color-correct" the tone of the skin with a pinky shade underneath my foundation, the same way you'd correct dark bags under your eyes.

PROPORTION

While bodies obviously vary wildly, there are things you can do to make your body look more "womanly" by altering the hip-to-shoulder ratio. Again, this is something drag queens do all the time by padding their hips and bums and cinching their waists. You can also get special bras with pockets for prosthetic breasts—they even sell these in stores for women who've had mastectomy surgery.

HAIR

A full head of lush hair is something we more commonly associate with women, so some trans women choose to grow their hair longer, have it cut into a traditionally female style, or get it dyed. Alternatively, a wig can go some way to lowering the hairline if having a slightly higher hairline is causing anxiety. Thanks to the internet, gorgeous human-hair, lace-front wigs are more affordable than they once were and—if cared for—will last for many years.

For Those Aiming for "Masculine"

HAIRCUT

Fairly obvious, but in the West, we code short hair as masculine. Go see a barber you trust, and get a stereotypical "men's" haircut, or—as ever—there are YouTube tutorials for cutting your own hair if you're feeling bold. Masculine styles tend to be shorter and blunter than feminine styles, which are usually more feathered and softer around the edges.

FACIAL HAIR

As women have been shamed for millennia into removing all facial hair, we very much associate facial hair with fellas. This can either be faked with makeup (ask your local drag king), or if you choose to take the hormone therapy route, some facial hair may develop.

BINDERS

This is a tricky subject and sort of boils down to what an individual finds more distressing: the dysphoria of chest tissue or a clingy compression garment. Binders aren't comfy, but some trans people wear a compression vest or a fitted tube top around the chest that smooshes the fat tissue down to create a flatter chest. It's recommended you get a binder that is made specifically for you and doesn't restrict your breathing. A very simple sizing tip is this: can you still take a deep breath while wearing it? If you can't, it's too tight. Medical professionals are divided on the potential harm a binder can do, but we must also factor in their potential mental health benefits. What is best for a person *overall*?

A person should bind for no more than six to eight hours at a time and shouldn't bind overnight. Take breaks if you get sweaty, hot, itchy, or uncomfortable. It goes without saying, but you'll need to wash your binder as often as you'd wash any undergarment.

Binders are not cheap. Sometimes people don't want to tell their parents they're binding, so some trans folk who no longer wear them rehome their old binders via social media.

DO NOT use bandages or tape to bind, and seek special advice if you're asthmatic or have any other respiratory conditions before starting to bind.

CLOTHES

Men's clothes are usually cut differently from those designed for women. Traditionally, men have smaller hip-to-waist ratios than women, so it's about wearing pants lower on the hip that don't cinch in at the waist or accentuate the curves. Cis men also tend to have much broader shoulders than cis women—an illusion that can be created with jackets and hoods.

PACKERS

Some cis people are obsessed with scrutinizing the general crotch area of trans people, so some transmasculine people like to "pack" their underwear with a prosthetic penis. And why not? Some folk like the way it looks and feels too. Remember that cis men's willies are usually only a couple of inches long when flaccid, so you don't need a python swinging around your pants. You can get "stand-to-pee" packers too, which enable a person to pee standing up.

For both transmasculine and transfeminine people, passing is an added thing to worry about. We wouldn't need to worry about passing so much if cis people weren't so bloody unkind to us in public. That said, don't let people shame you for *wanting* to pass or not: your gender, your body, your choice.

PICKING A NAME

There is a reason our parents choose our name when we're born: it's simply too big a responsibility to undertake on your own! So much pressure! How do you pick a single word that encapsulates everything you are? As babies, it's a stab in the dark that you'll suit your name, but as an adult, it's like trying on sweaters.

Choosing a new name is a **BIG DEAL** and a really wonderful and affirming part of the whole trans thing. So how can you find a name that suits you?

- If you're on good terms with your parents, why not ask them to help you choose a new name? Was there a name you'd have been called if you'd been assigned the right gender at birth?
- Explore the meanings of names. Feeling strong? Anders, Adira, and Bridget all mean "strength." Feeling powerful? Try Cyrene or Reginald.
- Do you have a favorite character in literature? Alice? Rue? Holden?
- Do you have a relative you'd be proud to name yourself after? A great-grandparent or similar?
- Nature can be very inspirational. What about Summer, Autumn, or Winter? Some people look to

fauna, like Fox, Lark, or Cat, while others go to flora: Lily, Ivy, Thorn.

- Mythological names are timeless (oh hai, Juno, Roman goddess of women). What about Hermes, Athena, or Troy?
- Friends often see us better than we see ourselves. Do they have any suggestions?
- There's no one more unique than you are. Why not *create* a word you feel suits your personality?
- If all else fails, 98 percent of trans men are called Finn or Flynn. **KIDDING, OBVIOUSLY!**

Here's the legal T with names. In the United States, each state has its own policy if minors want to change their name. Minors require the parental or guardian agreement of *all* parents or guardians, which has the potential to be bothersome. In Canada, each province and territory also has its own policy.

Loads more on the legal hilarity of being trans in chapter 13!

PRONOUNS

What will it be? You can choose from gendered (she/her, he/him) or nongendered pronouns (they/them, ze/zir).

Another slightly depressing disclaimer: people will absolutely get your pronouns wrong, whatever option you feel most comfortable with. Yes, it feels crappy **EVERY SINGLE TIME**, but it's another inevitable downside of the whole trans thing. What's important is that people are *trying* to get your pronouns right. You can instinctively tell when people are misgendering you maliciously and when they're making a genuine mistake. Our world is so gendered, it's so ingrained, that people do make honest mistakes. I'm afraid you'll have to get used to it in the first instance, but I find that people do adjust with time, and you'll get misgendered less and less as time passes.

Of course, people who use anything other than *he* or *she* pronouns are still fighting an uphill battle when it comes to society adjusting to their usage. There's nothing new about they/them pronouns, but people are very used to "they" to describe a group, and using they/them to describe an individual takes a little practice. Be patient (to a point) while your friends and family learn to do this. The more they do it, the better they'll get.*

---

* See? We use them all the time.

Why does it sting so much when people get it wrong? I suppose it can only be because you're working phenomenally hard to become the person you've always meant to be, and when people get it wrong, it suggests all your efforts aren't working or aren't being respected.

The good news is, by coming out, you've already proved you're an incredibly strong person, and if you got through that, you can get through some microaggressions.[†]

PAPERWORK

Now, this is where it starts to get tricky. While your family and friends might readily accept your new gender and/or identity, it might not be so easily managed in an official capacity.

Our lives are ruled by documentation:

- Birth certificate
- Bus or rail pass
- Bank accounts
- Passport
- Driver's license
- Doctors' and dentists' records
- School or college admissions

---

† We'll be exploring this term in the next chapter.

So while everyone might *call* you one name, *officially* you have another. At the time of writing, minors cannot legally change their gender, but they may be able to apply for a change of *name* if nothing else. Some forms of ID can be changed to reflect a binary change of gender (literally M to F and F to M) with written instructions from your family doctor. This, inevitably, only helps those going down "the medical route," which we'll cover in chapter 9.

It's pretty funny that there is so much fuss when it's actually fairly easy to apply for ID. For instance, your school *can* just change your name on their records. At school, my friend Vicky—who was only ever known as Vicky—was on the school records as Emma. She was called Emma at birth, but even as a tiny tot, her family called her by her middle name, Victoria, and the school accommodated that. All the teachers called her "Vicky." Easy. It really can be that simple *if* your school is supporting their trans students.*

As an adult, things are much easier—you don't need anyone's consent to change your legal identity. However, I do wish someone had warned me in advance how expensive all this paperwork can be. I was in a position of privilege and could afford the admin fees, but it was still irritating. In the United States, depending on the state, the cost for

---

* See how easy it is to use they/their pronouns?!

legally changing your name can range from $25 to $435. A new driver's license can cost up to $89, and a passport is currently $110. Costs are similar for Canada.

SCHOOL LIFE

I didn't figure out I was trans until I was a grown-up, but with the advent of the internet, much better representation in the media, and more education around trans issues, people are figuring out their identities at a younger age. That totally makes sense to me.

This means that, increasingly, young people will be questioning their identity, changing their identity, or taking the first tentative steps toward transition while still in school.

Charley Dean Sayers, an artist and model from London, did just that. She began to attend school as her authentic self when she was thirteen years old.

Like most trans girls, I have often found myself incessantly fixated with how other people may perceive my body. Going into sixth grade, I presented as male: I adopted "masculine" tendencies by cutting my long hair short and wearing the boys' school uniform as an attempt to suppress my identity through fear of being bullied. Two years later, when I finally plucked up enough courage to wear a skirt and a padded bra to school for the first time, I received polarizing reactions: while my close friends applauded me for my courage, I was met by blank stares by the rest of the school. Thankfully, my teachers were supportive of this decision. Academic staff were willing to adjust to my new pronouns while being respectful of my identity. They gave me access to the disabled toilets, but I had to ask a teacher for the key each time. I was always too anxious, so I ended up not using the loos until twelfth grade. They did, however, allow me to skip PE from middle school to my junior year. I thought this was great at the time, but I realized I couldn't touch my toes a few years ago and started to do some exercise!

The uncertainty surrounding my gender identity was relentless—so much so that on one occasion, it prompted a herd of students to harass me on my way home from school, with one girl going so far as to grab my bra to see if my breasts were real. During this time, I assumed that the abuse I received was a result of my ability to "pass" as female. I was under the impression that presenting an idealistic feminine persona would erase the question of what was in between my legs. I believe that trans women can find ourselves trapped within a system that demands us to change our bodies in order to make our existence more palatable for the people around us. I felt utterly hopeless having just recently started my hormone blockers; I knew it would be years until cross-sex hormones would even be discussed. I would tuck with duct tape, and with each second, the pain would intensify, serving as a reminder that my body was not "normal." I felt hyperaware of my severe discomfort, and this was largely compounded by the fact that no other person could relate. The sole purpose of my being became an attempt to feminize each aspect of myself; I began to believe the purpose and end goal of transitioning was to be attractive.

The large-scale adversity I faced during my transition has ultimately shaped who I am; as such, I have channeled this through my artwork, in which I reflect on being trans in a wider context that spans beyond the image portrayed of trans women in the media. This has compelled me to create self-portraiture that explores the complex and multifaceted nature of my gender identity through my use of film photography. Transgender identities are rarely well received if they are not in accordance with what society is comfortable with, especially in terms of passing culture. As a white, "passable" trans woman, I feel a certain responsibility to create work for trans women in society who aren't given the same privileges that I am.

Charley Dean Sayers, model and photographer

If you are planning to start your transition while you're in school, it's all about that one word I keep coming back to: **PATIENCE**. Nothing will change very quickly.

Ask yourself, what do you want to achieve? Do you want just your immediate friends and/or family to call you by a different name or use different pronouns? Or do you want the entire school community to respect a change in gender? The latter, clearly, will take more work.

Increasingly, teachers and schools are seeking guidance on how to accommodate trans and nonbinary students. Rarely do I visit a high school now where *someone* hasn't been through some form of gender change. As such, schools *should* have a policy in place. Again, what do you want? Do you want to ultimately use the girls'/boys' locker rooms for PE, or are you happy to use a disabled bathroom? While this is probably a bit discriminatory—you are a girl/boy if you say so—I'd have felt more comfortable with private changing, and with no official legal guidance in place regarding trans and/or nonbinary youth, you can see why schools might opt for this policy. Your school probably already has measures in place. Ask! Find out!

In the United States, Title IX is a federal law that makes sex discrimination illegal in most schools. Most courts that have looked at the issues have said that this includes discrimination against someone because they are transgender or because they don't meet gender-related stereotypes or expectations. In Canada, Bill C-16, passed in 2017, added trans protection to the Canadian Human Rights Act.

Like any other special need, your school has to

accommodate you to the best of their ability. They have to respect your decisions, names, and pronouns. That said, I've found that some schools are better than others at this.

As contradictory as it sounds, perhaps it's a case of you educating your school about the needs of trans and/or nonbinary students. Or it may be more efficient to move to a school that's more supportive. This choice is impacted by how "onside" your parents/caregivers are, clearly, but every year, students transfer schools for a hundred different reasons. It doesn't need to be a biggie.

Which leads nicely to my next point: as isolating as being trans can feel, remember you are **neither the FIRST nor ONLY** person to go through a gender transition while still in school. In fact, it's becoming fairly standard. I was a teacher from 2004 to 2011 and taught in elementary schools that had trans kids. All teachers want is what's right for each individual child to best support their learning. That's what school is for—to help you reach your potential.

PUBERTY

It's worth remembering that puberty is a trip for *everyone*. But for trans and/or nonbinary people, it can be an especially terrifying time. No one particularly enjoys their body rapidly changing, but it's very triggering to see your body change in a way that's at odds with how you visualize yourself. It's out of your control and can be scary.

This is why medical professionals sometimes prescribe puberty blockers (more in chapter 9)—they remove some of the anxiety surrounding the onset of puberty. That said, I did go through puberty and still went on to be very happy and very trans.

The onset of menstruation can also be troubling for everyone, but—again—even more so for trans and/or nonbinary people. Puberty blockers and, later, hormone replacement therapy don't automatically stop menstruation.

I always struggled with my periods, not just because they were painful physically but because they were also a mentally painful reminder of how uncomfortable I felt with my body. Every month, they brought with them a wave of dysphoria. I explored avenues to reduce my periods before coming out as trans because they were so heavy and unmanageable. A few years before I started transitioning, after becoming dangerously anemic due to heavy bleeding, my doctor advised me to have the Mirena coil fitted. The Mirena is a plastic device inserted into the womb that releases progesterone into the body to prevent pregnancy. However, it was also known to reduce or stop periods altogether. I remember the feeling of my periods eventually stopping. I counted myself so incredibly lucky, as that doesn't seem to be the case for everyone during their transition.

Jules Guaitamacchi, speaker and activist

Not all women have periods, and some men do. Some nonbinary people have them too. This is why we campaign for menstrual product machines and disposal bins in men's restrooms and appropriate sex education in schools.

ADULT LIFE

Can you remember those Richard Scarry books from when you were little? The ones with all the cute animals who went about doing jobs like baker, builder, and pilot? Well, find one of those books, because trans people are doing all those jobs!

As lovely as it would be if we could *all* be Laverne Cox or Kim Petras, the lifestyles of the rich and famous are tragically beyond the vast majority of us. Wherever there are people, there are trans people going about their daily lives. Know this:

 **THERE IS A FUTURE FOR YOU TOO.**

But I won't lie either. Historically, some transgender people have found it challenging out there, which is why so many choose to "live stealth." This is not because being trans or nonbinary is inherently tough but because some people out there are real assholes. And *that's* the T.

Just the other day, I was treated to two unrelated **ADULT** strangers sharing a little giggle together because they both "clocked" a transgender woman on the train. I can't repeat what my heroic friend Louis said to them, but it went something like "you pair of absolute *bleeping bleeps*."

Simply put, transphobia has made it difficult for some trans people to feel safe and confident in the workplace. The good news is that this is changing, with some companies training their staff on how to be more inclusive and mindful of trans staff and customers. I've delivered such training many times myself for big brands and organizations, such as Charlotte Tilbury, the Home Office, and various education authorities and arts venues.

Nevertheless, I am not going to lie to you and say, "Our society is A-OK with trans people, and you'll never experience transphobia in the workplace," because that's patently untrue.

REAL TRANS PEOPLE DOING CAREERS!

I'm a diversity and inclusion leader at a law firm. I work with businesses to help them become more inclusive and embrace diversity. I work on strategy and policy and report on matters such as the gender pay gap. I activate training and get people talking about sensitive topics and awareness raising. It also extends to adding stuff like gender identity boxes on data forms and having gender-neutral bathrooms.

Leng Montgomery, inclusion manager

I work for the National Police Air Service, and with my team, we provide helicopter support to police forces across the UK, twenty-four hours a day, 365 days a year. That might mean searching for missing or at-risk people or for suspects of crime using our high-powered camera or thermal imaging system. It might mean searching for and pursuing a wanted vehicle in cities or rural areas. It might mean landing in fields to pick up and move negotiators or dog units quickly to where they're needed. Or it could mean many other tasks—you never know what the day will bring. Operating the cameras, mission systems, six radios, and aircraft systems effectively and safely means working and training as a team that, per shift, consists of myself as the aircraft captain plus two police officers—a camera operator and a mission commander. My role is to ensure the aircraft is checked over each day and working as it should and that we're briefed and ready to go at any moment. Then to navigate through sometimes complex and busy UK airspace to where we're needed, including at night and in poor weather, and position the aircraft to make best use of the camera system. The police officers assist in navigating and aircraft safety, and once on scene, they mission-manage the task with units on the ground. We each have our roles and responsibilities but very much help each other out, knowing that our success is measured as a team.

Ayla Holdom, helicopter pilot

I've been a train operator on the London Underground for five years now. I've worked on the Piccadilly Line and Victoria Line, and my favorite part of the job is blowing the whistle for kids who wave at me from bridges on the outside sections of the track!

I'm genderqueer or transmasculine, and I've been using they/them pronouns for nearly a decade. In my job, it's quite flexible what uniform you wear, and people are free to mix and match, so I have always felt able to switch up my gender presentation as I see fit!

I hope to one day be a railroad signaler or to switch careers entirely and work with kids. I do really like my job, and I especially like that I don't have to hide who I am when I'm there.

CJ Kemal, train operator, Transport for London

As a filmmaker and writer, my day-to-day life can be quite variable. It ranges from planning out film projects we've taken on, including storyboarding, creating the right focus for the film, scriptwriting, scheduling in days for filming, doing the actual filming, and all the postproduction. This can mean long days and lots of travel, which also allows me to visit different places and see friends all over.

In terms of my writing or journalism, it's more about finding a quiet time to sit down with a nice drink, lighting a candle, and just writing, letting myself go into the topic I'm doing. It can be really challenging but also really rewarding when you see people share and connect with your writing.

Ugla Stefanía Kristjönudóttir Jónsdóttir
(Owl Fisher), filmmaker and journalist

Let's not pretend that transitioning isn't hard work. It's like having a whole other job on top of your actual job. But the good news is, you have your **WHOLE LIFE** to do both things. Don't feel too bad about not having your dream career while you're in the middle of sorting out your gender.

There's only so much you can do. But do take comfort that all around the world, people are living their best possible lives *and* being trans at the same time.

TRANSGENDER
HALL OF FAME

ALEX BERTIE

UK · THE VLOGGER VANGUARD

"As for not feeling trans enough: everybody is different. Don't focus on fitting into a box. Focus on being you and being happy and just doing whatever you need to be happy."

Given how difficult it has been for transgender people to rely on the mainstream media for fair coverage, it's no big surprise that the internet and social media have been vital in connecting and educating trans people. As a young trans man, Bertie is a role model to hundreds of thousands of followers on YouTube as well as being an author and activist.

8

THE PROBLEM IS OTHER PEOPLE

> The best thing about being trans is BEING TRANS. The worst thing about being trans is OTHER PEOPLE.
>
> **Munroe Bergdorf, model and activist**

In an ideal world, everyone would be equal. No one would be judged or discriminated against based on their gender, their sexuality, the color of their skin, their religion, their wealth, or their abilities. Not being funny, but the fact that I didn't pop out of the oven the way I'd have preferred is proof positive that we do *not* live in that ideal world.

The fact of the matter is:

NO ONE CHOOSES TO BE TRANS OR NONBINARY, BUT PEOPLE DO CHOOSE TO BE TRANSPHOBIC.

Think about it. Why would anyone *choose* a life with this much bloody admin? It's endless. Moreover, we know—instinctively—when we come out that things are going to be difficult. Yet we do it anyway, because it's the only shot we have at truly being ourselves. Sure, we get to choose what paths we take, but the feeling that you fundamentally disagree with the gender you were assigned at birth is absolutely out of your control.

But for cisgender people* to learn that trans and nonbinary people exist in the world and then have a problem with that? Well, that's a choice. You've considered the facts and decided to be prejudiced.

WELL, THIS IS A DOWNER.

---

* Or transgender. I know some binary trans people who are disparaging of nonbinary people and trans people who inexplicably don't support trans rights.

Yes, it is, but transphobia is very much a part of modern trans life. I think it would be super irresponsible of me to pretend it's all pumpkin spice lattes and baskets of kittens.

What's more helpful, I think, is to think about the ways in which transphobia could impact your life so you can take practical steps to avoid it and thus get on with the far more important business of being your most fabulous self!

IMPLICIT OR STRUCTURAL TRANSPHOBIA

The way our society is set up is inherently sexist and transphobic, but you already knew this. The world *assumes* you're cisgender unless you say otherwise, so unless you choose to tell the world how you feel, you're going to be misgendered from day one.

And that sucks.

The world assumes everyone is cisgender. It has been set up to work best for cis people. And so...

- Menstrual products are marketed toward women.
- Assumptions are made about "women's bodies" and "men's bodies."
- Maternity services are geared toward "women" and "mothers."

Trans people are—contrary to what some papers would have you believe—a tiny minority group. Yes, *nearly* all the people on the planet who menstruate are women. *Nearly* all the pregnancies in the world are going on inside women.

But not *all*. And the fact that the systems—for many decades—have ignored our little minority group has left us feeling homeless on our home planet. We are trained from a very young age to classify people into gendered groups. Boys and girls are asked to line up separately at school. Sometimes children will be divided by gender for PE or sex education. Then, as adults, we are greeted as "ladies and gentlemen" every time we step into a room.

CALM DOWN. I JUST WANT A BAG OF FRITOS, SHOPKEEPER.

These, my friends, are **MICROAGGRESSIONS**, a term used for outwardly "minor" verbal, behavioral, or structural indignities (intentional or unintentional) that communicate hostile, derogatory, or negative prejudicial slights and insults toward any group, particularly culturally marginalized groups.

Obviously, microaggressions don't only affect trans people. Any minority group is susceptible (and of course many trans people belong to other minority groups too). Don't believe me? Pop into your local Target or drugstore. Where are the hair products for Black people? Look at the subway map; why are only some stops accessible for wheelchair users? How is that fair?

I doubt cis, white, and nondisabled people even notice this is happening—all the time, every day. But people from minority groups do notice, because it leaves us feeling fundamentally misunderstood.

Different microaggressions will inevitably upset different people. Not all trans and/or nonbinary people are irritated by the same things. But if society was more mindful of these things, minority groups would be happier. Being "triggered" (a more polite way of saying "pissed off," in my opinion) by these "little things" doesn't make us "snowflakes."

While certain quarters mock minority groups for our

"whining," the daily drip-drip-drip of microaggressions can (at best) be exhausting and (at worst) take a serious toll on our mental health.

I'm not telling you these things to depress you. I'm telling you this because I wish I'd known. Seeing Kim Petras or Laverne Cox living their best red-carpet life can be slightly misleading. I do it too! I post my *highlights* to Instagram, *never* the days I wish I could hibernate in a salty sea cave for the rest of time.

The fact is, we are still pioneers. Trans people only started making serious inroads into mainstream culture in the last few decades. The world is still adjusting. For instance, in 2019, Stonewall Young Campaigner of the Year Ben Saunders convinced Always sanitary products to remove the female symbol from their packaging: a small thing that would have gone wholly unnoticed by cis people but means everything to trans men and/or nonbinary folk. Hopefully, together, we can make it easier for future generations.

EXPLICIT TRANSPHOBIA

As with any form of prejudice, transphobia exists on a sliding scale from the mildly ignorant to impolite to outright rudeness to flagrant discrimination.

1. "I HAVE CONCERNS..."

With all the garbage written in the tabloids, you almost can't blame cis people for having questions about the existence of trans and nonbinary folk in society. The press have fed people a set of "concerns" on a loop over the last few years.

- Are children being brainwashed?
- Are people mutilating themselves?
- Do trans women pose a risk to women and girls in single-sex spaces?

You almost can't blame people for adopting these concerns, but you *should*, because anyone with half a clue would educate themselves and interrogate what is spectacularly obvious prejudice.

It's hard to say for sure, but the last few years have seen an increasing number of negative stories about trans people. That is very concerning for us, because it makes us feel less safe in day-to-day life. I can only conclude that trans stories sell papers or they wouldn't bother. There are certainly a few well-placed and powerful journalists who use their considerable platforms to spread myths, rumors, and, again, their "concerns" about trans people.

It's easier to read scary headlines, I guess, than it is to read this entire book or, y'know, actually speak to a transgender person. I think an individual failure to challenge shocking headlines or bad journalism is a form of lazy transphobia.

APPLYING NEGATIVE STEREOTYPES TO A WHOLE MINORITY GROUP IS DEFINITELY PREJUDICED, I'M AFRAID.

2. NOSY QUESTIONS

This is a difficult one. Is a person firing a gazillion nosy, probing questions at you because they care about your experience or because they're just plain rude? At the end of the day, you don't owe anyone a crash course on being trans. They have Google, don't they?

I like to apply the granny rule: is that a question you'd ask your grandmother?

Deeply personal questions about your genitals, your

health care, your sex life, or your body are *not* something you'd discuss with a gran (I'd hazard). If people insist on asking nosy questions, I like to fire them back. "Oh, okay. Do you have a vagina?" This often serves to highlight how wildly inappropriate their questions are.

3. "MY HOLY BOOK SAYS..."

Oh, this old chestnut. When hateful people are desperate to think of themselves as good people, pure of heart, it's all too easy to defer to a third party. In this case, God. "Oh, it's not that I'm transphobic. It's my faith."

Now, some humans claim to have a direct line to gods of all faiths, and of course, some people believe various holy books are the word of God. But what do the holy books *actually* say on the issue of transgender people?

THE BIBLE says God created man and woman, and we shouldn't mess with God's creation. Fair, but since Eve was created from Adam's rib in Genesis, I'm not sure we should take it too literally. Jesus also preached that we should care especially for those born with birth defects. One modern interpretation of these teachings could include trans or intersex people, who were born this way. Okay, we don't need to be cared for—we're not sick—but I think Jesus would have respected trans and/or nonbinary folk and treated us with the same dignity. I'd say—if there was a

God—he or she or they wouldn't make mistakes. If I was religious, I'd assume they'd always planned this path for me.

JEWISH SCRIPTURE identifies six distinct genders: male, female, the androgynous (with male and female characteristics), the tumtum (whose biology is unclear), the ay'lonit (female at birth but develops male characteristics), and the saris (born male but adopt female traits).

THE KABBALAH—a sacred spiritual text—refers to people transitioning from one gender to another.

THE QUR'AN says nothing about trans people specifically, and there's no central governing body of Islam, but the Prophet Muhammad treated everyone with dignity and is said to have had a trans person in his household staff. So there.

Of course, if you want to hate something or someone badly enough, you could find support for it somewhere in a holy book. Let's not forget that the Bible declares both tattoos and shellfish abominations. Unless every Christian out there has sworn off shrimp and lobster, I really don't wanna hear homophobia or transphobia coming out of their mouths.

I find transphobes using very, very old texts, which have been translated and changed countless times to simply support their bigotry, especially tedious. Hate me because I'm a bitch, not because you're religious.

4. SLURS

Let's discuss the T word. You know the one, rhymes with "granny."

How I've argued with other trans people about this word! Some of my friends believe this word can be "reclaimed" by trans people and used as a term of endearment to describe oneself or friends.

The reason I *don't* do this is because I think it gives cis people tacit permission to also use the term.

Look at it this way: have you ever heard that word used in a complimentary way? No. It's used to describe crap hair, clothes, or makeup more often than not. It all adds to the notion that being trans is less than ideal. Not something I especially want to reclaim, if I'm honest.

And to get *really* serious: I greatly fear that the T word is the last word many a trans woman (and especially trans women of color) hear when they're being assaulted or, tragically, murdered.

If other people are using it, I think you can safely assume they're being transphobic. The same is true of *shemale* (which largely exists in pornography) and *shim*, which is just tacky.

All over the world, there are people making cheap jokes about people from minority groups. It's called "punching down," and that says more about a failed comedian than it does about the target.

5. ONLINE ABUSE

The internet, broadly speaking, is a very good thing. We all save loads on stamps, and we can learn things very quickly. However, the rise of social media, I'm starting to realize, has ruined our lives and is destroying society. While some people have always held fairly abhorrent beliefs, for the first few thousand years of civilization, we mostly didn't have to read their nonsense on a daily basis.

Understanding you can be as racist, homophobic, or indeed transphobic as you like on social media platforms and **NEARLY ALWAYS** get away with it, people have been emboldened to say things they'd rarely dare say on the street, at school, on the train, or at the office. It's real easy to be anonymous online. Where are the consequences?

This has meant that trans and nonbinary people can become targets of online abuse. Users can be the victims of mockery, constant challenges, or attempts to engage in discussions or debates about trans life. *But what about...? But what do you say to...?*

These attempts to undermine trans and/or nonbinary people are tiresome to say the absolute least. Trans people—especially trans women—may also be harassed by (mostly) men who regard them as sexual objects.

I'm not going to tell you how to live your life, but I have a blanket **BLOCK AND REPORT** policy for people who either send transphobic abuse or have account names or bios that indicate they exist only to engage in transphobia.

So goes the old saying, "Don't roll in the mud with pigs. The pig likes it, and you both get dirty." I think, for some, online transphobia is a very sad hobby. If you get into arguments too, you basically have the same hobby as them. You're spending your leisure time on transphobia.

Don't give it oxygen. Let it wither and die.

That said, if you're being targeted for abuse, screen-grab everything. You can take this evidence to your teachers or even the police. Online harassment is a **CRIMINAL OFFENSE.** Transphobes—including some very high-profile ones—have been cautioned by the police over their online behavior.

WHAT'S A TERF?

You've almost certainly heard this phrase. It means trans exclusionary radical feminist. It's used to describe transphobic people who claim feminism as an excuse to criticize us or restrict our human rights. Their argument is that the presence of (usually) trans women is a threat to cis women.

Hopefully, we all recognize this as a snide way of suggesting trans women are dangerous. This is very transphobic, obviously.

I do not call them TERFs. Why? I am a **FEMINIST**—someone

who wants political, economic, and social equality for women and nonbinary folk. All my friends are feminists too. So I don't see why transphobes get to be called feminists.

You see, in the struggle for equality, women and nonbinary people from minority groups have further to go than cis, white, straight, nondisabled women. This clearly includes transgender women, as we don't (yet) have the same rights as cis women. There's work left to do. If feminism isn't for every woman, it's not feminism.

Also, if you use TERF in a Twitter debate, transphobes *always* derail your argument and turn it into a discussion called "TERF is a slur!"—and that's your mentions gone.

6. DISCRIMINATION

This is when people take their prejudices against groups and put them into action. In reality, this can take lots of different forms:

- Refusing to provide services, like letting trans people stay in hostels, hotels, or rented accommodation.
- Refusing to hire trans people or let them enroll in courses.
- Passing over trans people for bonuses or promotion.
- Barring entry to public spaces, including changing rooms or toilets.

The good news is that many transgender people in the United States are protected under state laws. However, state laws don't always translate into actual fair treatment. If someone does discriminate against you, you are often legally allowed to challenge them.

Doesn't mean it feels very nice though. I was once discriminated against for a career opportunity overseas, and while I *could* have lawyered up, who actually does that? I didn't have the funds, so I did what I could—I called them out online. The power of shaming is real.

A good deal of the discourse around trans people is around single-sex spaces, so let's discuss that here: particularly toilets, changing rooms, and prisons.

BATHROOM BILL

Here's what some people think: if we allow trans and nonbinary people to change their ID to better reflect their gender, chaos will reign, tipping the world into an apocalypse.

Oh, it's not that they're *transphobic*. They *like* trans people. It's just that if we simplify the process of changing gender, a scary cis male pervert—let's call him Bathroom Bill—will exploit these changes in the law to his own nefarious ends. According to them, if we let trans women in the ladies' washrooms, Bathroom Bill will creep in and assault cis women and girls.

Let's be very clear: cis men are scary. Before you start screaming #notallmen, I'll explain. Cis men can be scary, because we know from lots of data that some cis men do, sadly, assault women and girls.

However, there is almost *no* data to suggest this happens in public toilets or changing facilities. In fact, statistically, a woman is most likely to be sexually or physically assaulted by a partner or ex-partner.

The argument goes that if we do make it easier for trans people to change their gender ID, that'll all change, and the Gap changing rooms will rapidly come to resemble *A Nightmare on Elm Street*.

But **HERE'S THE T.** Binary trans people can already apply for new ID long before they have any medical interventions. In some places in the United States, people can already change their gender without needing a doctor's official approval, and guess what? They haven't seen any cases of cis men pretending to be trans. Like, why would a sexual predator go to the trouble to do all that paperwork? Think about it: Is Bathroom Bill, dangerous criminal, going to engage with a legal process involving ID, paperwork, and fees before doing his criminal acts? Like, really?

Oh, and one other thing:

NO ONE CHECKS YOUR PASSPORT BEFORE YOU POOP.*

Since when did you have your ID checked in a public toilet or locker room? It simply doesn't occur. Trans people have been peacefully going about their public lives for decades. You've been sharing public spaces with trans and/or nonbinary people your entire life.

In reality, people suggesting that letting trans people live is in some way dangerous are being transphobic. Denying a minority group very basic rights is always a sign of prejudice, *especially* if there is no evidence to suggest those rights would truly impact on anyone else.

BUT THE BAD ONES!

If you look at any demographic group in society—men, women, children, people of color, trans people, gay people,

---

* Unless you're pooping on a plane: the unisex bathroom no one has an issue with.

parking enforcement officers—there will always be a percentage of bad apples.

But you really know you've arrived in a minority group when the actions of a miniscule fraction of people are attributed to a whole group.

I could name two...or maybe three...trans people throughout history who are very bad people who've done very bad, very criminal things. Yes, we should lock them away (in the correct prison and for the appropriate amount of time) until they have been rehabilitated. What we shouldn't do is use those cases to insinuate *all* trans people are very bad people who might do very bad, very criminal things...and yet this happens with alarming regularity.

To me, that's like saying we should fear doctors because of Harold Shipman or nurses because of Beverley Allitt.* It makes no sense, and if people are attributing the actions of *individuals* to a *group*, you're dealing with a certified bigot.

7. VIOLENCE

It is important for trans and nonbinary people to know we are vulnerable but not to be ruled by fear.

With this in mind, it's important to discuss the violence that some trans people faced and continue to face. We know

---

* Both notorious murderers, true-crime fans.

that transphobic hate crimes are on the rise in the United States and Canada, surging 20 percent in just one year.* Worse still, in 2019, 331 transgender and gender-diverse people (that we know of) were unlawfully killed around the world.† When you consider what a tiny fraction of the population we are, that's way too many. Most of those victims were trans women of color. Some of them were also sex workers.

In its worst form, transphobia kills. We have to know this.

But trans people are not responsible for our untimely deaths. We must go out there and be ourselves, live our lives, and live gloriously. Transphobes want us to live in the shadows, but living in the shadows makes us easier to target. What we can do is look out for our trans siblings, keep tabs on our friends, lend them money for cabs, watch them get home safe, and talk to one another about men who seek to hurt trans women.

We must be *mindful*, not *fearful*.

It's also good to keep reporting any form of violence—verbal or physical—to the police. No force wants dreadful

---

* Dan Avery, "Anti-Transgender Hate Crimes Soared 20 Percent in 2019," NBC News, November 17, 2020, https://www.nbcnews.com/feature/nbc-out/anti-transgender-hate-crimes-soared-20-percent-2019-n1248011.

† "TMM Update Trans Day of Remembrance," TransRespect versus Transphobia, November 11, 2019, https://transrespect.org/en/tmm-update-tdor-2019.

hate crime statistics, and consistent reporting will encourage the authorities to take prevention more seriously.

I remember at the start of my transition, I went with my blokey dad (hi Dad) to B&Q [a home improvement store] to get some paint to decorate my bedroom. I'd just started presenting as female in public, and I lived in a constant state of anxiety and fear. Transphobia was a normal part of my everyday life. I looked kinda bad because I was still learning how to do my makeup—it's ironic that I was going to buy paint, because I looked like I did my makeup with wall paint—so I'd get stared at a lot. I vividly remember how I felt walking into that store that day, knowing I'd face some sort of abuse with it being a super masculine environment. As expected, I was stared at, laughed at, and commented at. I remember just as vividly how I felt when I left the store and the thought that went through my head: I can't wait till the day I can go somewhere like B&Q and not get stared or laughed at. It seemed like a million years away.

Over the years, I practiced my makeup (I still accidentally go a bit heavy sometimes and look like a *Drag Race* contestant). I got laser hair removal. I took hormones. I practiced feminizing the way I talk and walk. I grew my hair. I had a bit (okay, a lot) of surgery, and I worked on my confidence and got to a point where I was so sure of myself, I didn't care if anyone stared at me or laughed at me because I loved myself.

Anyway.

Guess who went to B&Q the other day? Me!

And guess who didn't get laughed at or stared at (apart from a guy in the lighting aisle who was defo checking me out)? Me.

And guess who wouldn't have believed you if you told them this would happen a couple of years ago? Me.

As I walked out of the store, I got emotional and started to cry. I remembered that time I came with my dad years before and how I would have given literally anything just to blend in. It felt like an impossible dream. I couldn't even imagine how it would feel because it felt so unrealistic. But the funny thing is, it's become so normal now that I've almost forgotten that feeling of fear and anxiety I'd carry around with me every single day early in my transition. Kinda like a bad dream you forget when you wake up. I'm not sharing this to boast about how passable I am—I still get clocked. I'm sharing this in case you're where I was. You might be reading this at a point in your transition where you feel (or rather, are made to feel by idiots) like a freak show. You might feel like it'll always be that way and that you'll never get to a point where you're happy with your body or your place in society. You might feel a million miles from where you want to be, but in those moments, remind yourself of the million miles you have walked to be where you are now. Your B&Q moment is coming, baby. You're a lot closer than you think.

You got this.

Charlie Craggs, Nail Transphobia founder

TRANSGENDER HALF OF FAME
INDYA MOORE

USA · THE POLITICAL POSER

"Even before *Pose*, I was involved in activism and advocating for my community in various ways. I didn't see that stopping with my entry into [the entertainment] industry, but people are going to be afraid of what you're going to say. I'm going to bump heads with people that benefit from the oppression that they put trans people through."

Moore, a nonbinary actor who uses they/them pronouns, shot to fame playing sex-worker-turned-model Angel in the groundbreaking TV show *Pose*. Moore uses their platform wisely to address white supremacy and even wore jewelry featuring the faces of those who'd died as victims of transphobic violence to a Hollywood award show.

9

DOCTOR, DOCTOR! I THINK I'M TRANSGENDER!

Recently, ill-advised and overpriced holiday vacation packager Center Parcs insisted their policy was to bar trans women (they didn't even mention trans men, because trans men are all but forgotten) from changing rooms unless they had undergone "a full transition."

Is this like a "full English breakfast"? At some point, will people bring me eggs?

BISH, WE ALL KNOW THAT'S NOT HAPPENING.

I want to mention this up front, because there is a long-held belief that transition can only be completed, video-game style, with what we now call **GENDER CONFIRMATION SURGERY.** Some tabloids *still* insist on calling it "sex change surgery."

You may have also heard it called, colloquially, "bottom surgery."

This is simply not the case. Transition, in all its infinite forms, is a lifelong process. I will be trans forever, regardless of how many surgeries I have. It describes the journey my life undertook. There are as many ways to transition as there are trans people.

For many, doctors and hospitals and surgeries are not the right approach. Feeling at odds with your birth gender does not automatically mean you'll want or need medical intervention. We already heard Jamie Windust tell us how

they knew they didn't want to go down that path. But for some, altering our physical bodies both reduces dysphoria and increases joy and self-worth. People tend to focus on the former, but looking the way I do hasn't just removed sadness. It has actively boosted my happiness. Well, of course it has—I now look pretty much how I've wanted to look in my head since I was, like, four. And of course, sometimes people who identify as nonbinary *also* want hormone therapy and surgeries. It's not a mutually exclusive thing.

The general vibe here is that everyone should be able to look how the hell they want to look and the way that makes them happiest. Makes sense, right? But the choices you make about surgeries have zero bearing on how trans you are.

This isn't just an ideological thing. Depending on your age, your location, and your finances, even the option of surgeries may be a great many years away. The cost of private treatment for people without insurance is well out of reach for most mortals. So given that pretty much all trans people are in it for the very long haul—years and years—we can't say someone at the start of their journey is any less valid than someone who's gone through surgery. That's just not fair.

The medical pathway is different for minors and adults. In the UK (for the time being), we have a National Health

Service (NHS) that provides both groups with free gender-affirming health care, paid for through taxes. As a UK citizen, that's the system I went through, so it's the one I know. If you reside elsewhere, the systems in place to support you will vary wildly. Unfortunately, we also have to bear in mind that any support we have fought for over the last few decades can be repealed at a moment's notice. With our rights about medical treatment continually in flux, the best advice I can offer is to

SPEAK TO YOUR LOCAL TRANS PEOPLE.

They will know. They will also know tricks and short-cuts for speeding up your access to treatment, if that's what you want.

In 2014, I thought I knew it all because I'd spoken to my cisgender therapist and cisgender family doctor. Well, let's just say, I'd have saved myself a lot of time if I'd gone out for dim sum with a group of trans people. If you can't physically meet other trans people in your area, use the internet. There are forums and groups on social media that will keep you informed.

TRANS YOUTH

For people under eighteen, I always think the first port of call is an adult you trust. This could be a teacher, librarian, school counselor, or family doctor. Hopefully they'll steer you in the right direction. There's online information in chapter 17 too. Don't forget, if you do come up against resistance from professionals who tell you "it's a phase" or similar, you have every right to seek out a different doctor or nurse.

If you do wish to consider the medical route, in the United States and Canada, you will generally need permission from your parent or guardian to do a hormonal or surgical transition before you are eighteen years old.

You should also expect a period of therapy or counseling. What doctors are looking for is evidence that an individual's experience of gender dysphoria is **INSISTENT**, **CONSISTENT**, and **PERSISTENT**: basically that your feelings are ongoing and are unlikely to change in the future. This isn't because they're *doubting* you so much as assessing whether or not to invest time and money in your treatment. It's about figuring out what the right path for you is. Because, don't forget, the medical route is not the only route to happiness in your body.

After a whole heap of waiting, talking, waiting, and more talking, you may be offered **HORMONE BLOCKERS**. This medication—more formally called gonadotropin-releasing hormone analogues—is the holy grail for many trans youth. They reduce the dysphoric terror of going through the wrong puberty and watching your body change in ways you might not want.

Depending on what state or province you live in, you may be able to start taking blockers earlier than the age of sixteen. However, several states in the United States have introduced or are considering legislation that would prohibit medical treatment for children who may be transgender, including the use of pubertal blockers.[*]

The Endocrine Society and the World Professional Association for Transgender Health support the use of puberty blockers for kids who want to delay or prevent unwanted physical changes. The U.S. Food and Drug Administration has approved puberty blockers for children who start puberty at a young age.[†]

All medicines come with side effects, so it's about balancing the **HORROR** of gender dysphoria against any potential side effects.

---

[*] Joshua D. Safer, "Controversial Pubertal Blocker Legislation May Bring Unintended Consequences for Children," *Endocrine Today*, February 17, 2020, https://www.healio.com/news/endocrinology/20200217/controversial-pubertal-blocker-legislation-may-bring-unintended-consequences-for-children.

[†] "Puberty Blockers," Children's Hospital St. Louis, https://www.stlouischildrens.org/conditions-treatments/transgender-center/puberty-blockers.

Puberty blockers can be a really useful pause button while you figure things out.

A lot of people have a lot of things to say on the use of blockers, but *concerns* and *opinions* aren't doing anything to soften the anxiety and depression experienced by young trans people. Puberty blockers do have an impact on mental well-being and provide more positive outcomes. I spoke to model and artist Charley Dean Sayers, who opted to take blockers during her teen years. She said, "Puberty blockers allowed me to grow into the person I am. I don't know if I would have survived without them. The only scary thing about puberty blockers is how misinformed everyone is about their use and effect."

Please remember that initiating hormone treatments is *not* a magic bullet. Dysphoria won't vanish overnight. If you are depressed and anxious, that may well continue to some degree.[‡] What hormone treatment may give you is some sense of control over the uncontrollable, but remember, you can take control of your life and gender in nonmedicinal ways too: by changing your name, pronouns, clothes, hair, and so on.

---

‡ And those conditions may require medical attention of their own.

Once you're sixteen or seventeen or have been on blockers for about two years, you might be started on "cross-gender" hormones if you're still keen to pursue a medical transition. So in transmasculine peeps, this would be **TESTOSTERONE**, and in transfeminine ones, **ESTROGEN**.

WHAT TO EXPECT WHEN YOU'RE EXPECTING HORMONE TREATMENT

As with blockers, starting your hormone replacement therapy (HRT) is not going to magically change your life overnight.

Both testosterone and estrogen are powerful hormones and can create dramatic changes in the human body—but it takes time. Here's what you can *realistically* expect to happen.

Taking Estrogen	Taking Testosterone
Softer skin	Less soft skin
Reduced body hair growth	Increased body and facial hair
Reduced sex drive	Increased sex drive
Redistribution of fat in the body to produce a more "feminine" shape	Redistribution of fat to create a more "masculine" shape
Some breast and nipple growth	Clitoral growth
Decrease in genital size	Change to facial shape
Potential mood swings	Potential mood swings
Possible infertility	Menstruation may eventually stop
	Voice will become lower

But... (and it's a big butt, etc.) HRT is a very inexact science. Very little actual research has been done on the effect of hormones on the transgender body. We just know that this is what is *likely* to happen if one takes "cross-sex" hormones.

For some, the treatment works quite quickly and with noticeable physical changes; in others, the changes are minimal and slow to develop. And bear in mind that testosterone is a more "powerful" hormone than estrogen, so the effects can be more apparent in trans men and its handiwork harder to undo in trans women.

This is why "have patience" is the absolute best advice I can give. Nothing in Transland happens quickly.* HRT is a lifelong commitment. For as long as I want to look the way I do, I'll be popping those little pills, although the most apparent changes take place over the first two years or so of treatment. This obviously varies from person to person.

Estrogen comes in the form of pills, gels, or patches, while testosterone is either given as an injection, a cream or gel, or—in rare cases—a tablet (although this is the least effective method). Trans women—if "preop"—usually also receive an antiandrogen injection every three months (delivered by a nurse) to keep the pesky effects of testosterone at bay. These injections will be stopped if the testicles are removed surgically.

It's important to be realistic about what *won't* happen once you're on the hormones too. The voices of those

---

* I swear my boobs are still growing after four years, but that could just be all the cake, tbh.

taking estrogen won't change: that requires vocal therapy or at-home practice with the help of apps or even YouTube tutorials. It's also the case that body hair doesn't magically drop out. Facial hair in particular can be a nightmare to get rid of if you reached adulthood before starting your transition and will require many months of laser treatment or electrolysis to remove.* Both of these treatments are expensive (if sought privately) and painful. Usually trans people have laser first, as it's less painful, and then electrolysis to remove any stubborn hairs that refuse to be zapped.

For folks who do take testosterone, chest tissue—if developed—won't vanish. Some trans men and nonbinary folk use **BINDERS** to flatten their silhouette—although these are very uncomfortable to wear—or opt to have "top surgery" to remove the chest tissue.

The first changes driven by testosterone (skin, increased sex drive, and deeper voice) can happen in a few weeks or months, while some changes (body hair and beard growth) can take many months or even years to occur, although this varies dramatically from person to person. Taking testosterone will usually cause changes to the menstrual cycle: some find their bleeding gets lighter; some find their menstruation

---

* Some sessions of laser hair removal can be claimed for free on the NHS, but this usually isn't enough for full, effective hair removal.

comes and goes less regularly; some find that it stops completely. This is why we shouldn't think of menstruation as something that only affects women. That association can turn a monthly trip to buy sanitary products into a dysphoria horror show. Of course, any menstruating person has the option to control their cycle with birth control as well.

PRIVATE HEALTHCARE

In the United States, people rely on health insurance through their work or their parents' work or pay privately. This is usually very, very expensive. This means there is a growing divide between trans people from wealthy backgrounds and those from poorer backgrounds. I don't have to tell you the world isn't a fair place.

Even in countries where free healthcare is available, people can choose to buy private health care if they are very wealthy and fortunate. Again, this isn't fair, obviously, but the world is not fair. We can all strive to make the world fairer, but we also want to do that striving while receiving appropriate health care. It's really hard to be a "trans activist" when you can't get out of bed for gender dysphoria.

So let's not judge any trans person who might opt for private health care. It isn't just for Lord and Lady Transworthy either; many normal, hard-working transgender people save and save for years or put together crowdfunding campaigns to afford private health care.

Trans allies reading this book: I'd urge you to donate as much as you can to crowdfunding campaigns set up by trans people. Honestly, that's the most tangible support you can give.

Realistically, private treatments start at about $350 for a laser hair removal session (and an adult trans woman would need multiple sessions) and end up in the tens of thousands of dollars for bigger surgeries requiring anesthetics and nights in private clinics.

THE OP

Any self-respecting trans person should be, like, LOL at that phrase. To cis people, that exclusively means **HAVE YOU HAD IT CHOPPED OFF, LOVE?** To trans people—intellectuals—we know that there's a myriad of surgical nips and tucks we can opt for if we have the inclination and/or money.

So it's not a case of "the op"; it's a case of "the ops," again, if you want 'em.

Surgery	Description
Top surgery/bilateral mastectomy	Some people with unwanted chest tissue may opt to have this surgically removed.
Hysterectomy and salpingo-oophorectomy	Some trans folk may also choose to have the uterus, fallopian tubes, and ovaries removed.
Phalloplasty and scrotoplasty	This is the construction of a penis and scrotum (sometimes with penile or testicular implants) using tissue from the existing genitalia and, usually, forearm. The patient—in time—may be able to pee through the penis and have penetrative sex. This is a hugely complex procedure often requiring multiple operations. While the procedure is always improving, it still doesn't have a 100 percent success rate.
Breast augmentation	If dissatisfied with breast growth on hormone therapy, some trans people choose to have breast implants.
Metoidioplasty	This is the surgical reconstruction of an enlarged clitoris to function like a penis. Metoidioplasty is a slightly less risky, more straightforward operation than phalloplasty, as you're working with tissue that's already in place. A person can pee through the new penis but is potentially less capable of sexual penetration due to the slightly smaller-than-average size of the penis. Sexual stimulation is still achievable.
Facial feminization	This refers to a series of operations that can be employed to make a face "more feminine." This can include rhinoplasty (nose job), chin or jaw augmentation, brow contouring (softening the brow), hairline lowering, or hair transplantation.

Surgery	Description
Body shaping	Some trans people also choose to create a more "feminine shape" by having implants or fat redistribution. This surgery, like any surgery, can be a lot more risky than it seems.
Vaginoplasty	A complicated operation in which skin and nerves from the penis and scrotum are used to create a vagina, vulva, and clitoris. This operation is followed by a lengthy period of dilation to ensure the vagina doesn't seal over. This means inserting a dildo several times a day while healing. Following the operation, most patients report sexual sensation and can achieve orgasm.
Orchidectomy	Sometimes trans people choose to keep their penis but remove their testes, removing the need for antiandrogen injections.

Let's say this one really clearly for anyone reading this book with an intent to pull it to pieces:

TRANS CHILDREN ARE NOT HAVING ANY OF THESE SURGERIES IN THE UNITED STATES OR ELSEWHERE.

It just doesn't happen. Yes, lots of trans youth *want* these things once they're adults, but—like the rest of us—they'll have to wait.

OP OPTIONS

The decision about whether or not to pursue surgery is totally down to each individual transgender person. In the olden days, it was assumed that "transitioning" was essentially a surgical procedure and that all trans people would opt for surgery. These days, it's very much a choice.

A good doctor will talk with their patient about their goals and feelings. It's important to bear in mind that operations are zero fun. All major surgery comes with health risks, and the recovery periods are extensive: you may well be sore, bruised, discharge-y, and swollen for up to a year postop. A good doctor will always talk you through the potential risks and side effects well ahead of surgery. On the flipside, once it's done, it's done, and you can get on with the rest of your life.

I certainly can't advise other people on whether to push for surgeries. I think you know how you want your body to be in your heart of hearts. The good news is, there's no rush. A good friend of mine was scheduled for surgery and then decided she wanted more time to think it through. The doctors were totally fine with this and understood her decision, telling her she can get a new referral if she decides to proceed in the future.

What's definitely true is that trans people who have surgery are no more or less valid than those who do not. No one is "more trans" or "more committed" than anyone else. It's *your* body and *your* choice.

> I postponed my gender reassignment surgery because keeping my penis didn't discredit my womanhood. The longer I lived in my desired gender identity, the more I understood that my "transness" had always been there and always would, regardless of my genitalia. I decided to own and honor my truth, rather than follow a script that was written by someone else.
>
> **Anonymous, London**

The talented writer and activist Juno Roche wrote a whole book about her relationship with her body following surgery some years ago.[*]

> I suspect, like many other trans women, femmes, and gender-nonconforming people, that as I lay down on the operating table and counted down backward to sleep, I believed I would wake up on the other side of surgery with a perfect vagina that would complete my

---

[*]   Juno Roche, *Trans Power: Own Your Gender* (London: Jessica Kingsley, 2019).

life. People often say, "it's the final part of the gender-journey jigsaw." That our "womanhood," our "femininity" will be sited within our new perfectly realistic genitalia.

When I did emerge from the haze of painkillers and in-and-out sleep, a nurse very sweetly handed me a handheld makeup mirror (very Victorian!) and suggested I take a peek at my perfect pussy.

I think my words were, "What the actual f***!"

To be completely honest, in so many ways, the whole process was perfect, but for the first few days, it just resembled a very angry, cerise monkey's bottom, the kind that gets pushed upward in nature programs toward people watching television while munching on KFC.

Over the next few days, the monkey's bottom subsided, and with love, people started to tell me that it "looked great," "just like the real thing." I showed it to a friend, and they said to me that, "no one would ever know that it wasn't a real vagina."

While discussing aftercare, my surgeon suggested that I could grow a luxuriant bush of pubes to cover the stitch lines that ran down either side of my vulvic area. Rather than seeing that as a workable 1970s pubic solution, it made me feel angry about the apparent need I now had to cover up my truth and to hide my scars. Weren't the scars real? Weren't they the things that defined this part of my upcycled journey?

I felt sad that people interpreted this surgical process as me moving from never feeling like a boy or a man to now simply looking "real." How could I comfortably occupy being "like the real thing" when I'd have to start that journey by hiding my scars?

I realized that I couldn't occupy a vagina that just looked real. It wasn't deep enough for me, metaphorically speaking. I never wanted to hide my truth. I became proud of my trans identity through my genital upcycling.

I changed the dynamic and embraced the materiality of my genitals—an upcycled cock and balls that really does look like a vagina. They are brilliant, a work of art, a trans work of art.

A transgina!

A space I fully occupy, a space that speaks volumes about my desire for comfort in my own body rather than chasing a body deemed to be good enough to pass in a world that is all too ready to reject us for trying too hard anyway. I only hope that generations of trans people to come will ask more questions around surgery, better questions, less about looking real and more about safety and pleasure.

Juno Roche, author and campaigner

At the end of the day, every single person on the planet has a complicated relationship with their body. In the age of Instagram, how could they not? We're bombarded with notions of what a "perfect" body should look like every day.

What I'm saying is, if you're unhappy with your body, there isn't a surgical procedure to remove unhappiness. If only there was!

That said, with each surgery I've had, I've *preferred* my body. Like, I'm still an anxious mess a lot of the time, but I *prefer* my dinky new nose.

Make of that what you will.

TRANSGENDER HALL OF FAME
THOMAS BEATIE

USA · THE FOUNDING FATHER

"I have a very stable male gender identity. I see pregnancy as a process, and it doesn't define who I am. It's not a male or female desire to want to have a child—it's a human desire. I'm a person, and I have the right to have my own biological child."

In 2008, images of Beatie cradling his unborn child in utero shocked a world that, for the most part up to that point, didn't really know transgender men existed. After appearing on *Oprah* to discuss the discrimination he and his wife had encountered, global education moved forward.

10

LOVE AND ROMANCE

When I first told my mum that I was transgender, her first response—the very first sentence that popped out—wasn't "Oh no!" It was, "But how will you find a boyfriend?"

I can't lie; that thought had occurred to me too. You can't be what you can't see, and I'd never seen or known a transgender woman to have a lasting, successful relationship with anyone, in the media or in real life. I made peace with that. I decided—after many failed relationships—that it was more important to be the most authentic version of myself than it was to have a boyfriend. As RuPaul has said many times, "If you can't love yourself, how the hell you gonna love somebody else?"

I'd go so far as to say that the *reason* I couldn't make a relationship work before I transitioned was because falling in love means getting to know someone at their very core, and I was hiding my true self from everyone, even myself.

I was so sure that the romantic plotline of my story was

finished that I was really very unprepared when I learned that there's loads of love, romance, and sex out there for transgender people—assuming you want it!

SEXUALITY

In the easiest possible terms, sexuality defines who you'll eventually go to bed *with*, and gender is who you go to bed *as*.

Having said that, nothing is ever black and white when you're dealing with two things as flipsy-flopsy fluid as sexuality and gender. Both of these variables are liable to change over time. Some people have very clear notions of who they are and who they like. For others, it's less well defined. Your sexuality, like your gender, is your business, and everyone is valid. There's not really a lot you can do about either—gender and sexuality are *not* "choices," as some nutjobs would have you believe.

This is another reason why it's so important for the entire LGBTQ+ community to work together. You can't remove the T, because a lot of trans people are also gay, lesbian, or bisexual. Trans people experience homophobia, and gay and lesbian people experience transphobia. We absolutely *must* work together to eradicate hatred.

GENDER and **SEXUALITY** are often (inaccurately) conflated.

They are two separate concerns. Every last person on earth needs to ponder *who they are* and *who they like*. It shouldn't take long. Have a go now during your coffee break.

Cool. How was that?

If only it was that easy! Desire is a wibbly-wobbly sex cloud one has little control over. Just when you think you're *definitely* straight, someone of your gender rocks your world or vice versa. Some people find transgender or nonbinary lovers a challenge to their preconceived sexuality, although they needn't be.

At the end of the day, we like who we like, but we do get to decide how to define ourselves in terms of both gender and sexuality. No one else gets to dictate your identity.

So why bother with labels at all? If we're all constantly in flux, why bother drawing lines in the sand? At the end of the day, I suppose it's just faster and easier. If you're at a packed house party, entering into a lengthy monologue about the tyranny of labels isn't going to go down as well as a quick "I'm gay, babes! You?"

It's a pick 'n' mix of labels out there. Here are some you've definitely heard of and some you might not have.

- **GAY:** Used by male and female same-sex couples. This obviously includes trans men who date men and trans women who date women.

- **LESBIAN:** Used by female same-sex couples. This obviously includes trans women who date women.
- **BISEXUAL:** Someone who's attracted to people of two or more genders.
- **PANSEXUAL:** Very similar to bisexual, but for some, that word inherently suggests a binary (hello, bi), so "pansexual" reinforces attraction to ALL genders, including nonbinary ones.
- **ASEXUAL:** Asexual people, though they might have sex for lots of reasons, typically have little or no *desire* to have sex or sexual relationships.
- **AROMANTIC:** Asexual people might do all the lovey-dovey bits without the sex. Aromantic people have no desire to do the coupling up stuff but may still want sex.
- **QUEER:** An umbrella term used to position oneself as something other than straight or cisgender.*

---

* I'm not here to sell identity, but I found great strength in my queer identity. As a white, straight, trans woman who mostly passes, it's important to me that I'm not assimilated into the dominant straight, cis culture. Being queer allows me to express that quickly.

When I joined the Royal Air Force, I was just out of university and had not yet transitioned... I hadn't even come out to myself yet. It was before I was married, but I was already dating my future wife. We've been married for ten years now (this month), and we were together for seven years before that. Wren's always been my biggest ally. Having such a deeply supportive partner was wonderful given how many years I was afraid to speak about [being transgender], afraid to even think about it.

Ayla Holdom, helicopter pilot

IF I LIKE TRANS MEN OR TRANS WOMEN, DOES THAT MAKE ME GAY?

Not automatically, no.

Like I said earlier, the only person who gets to define your identity is you.

On a practical level, there's very little you can do about who you like. You either do or you don't. I am (historically) only attracted to men, and that absolutely includes trans men. Why? Well, they look like men, smell like men, sound like men... They are men! I would still describe myself as heterosexual.

As you'll learn in this chapter, sex does not begin and end with a penis going inside a vagina. It's so much more than that. I doubt anyone is attracted to disembodied penises or vaginas. That would be gross.

We are attracted to *people*.

The bottom line is this: I *really* don't think my gay male friends would ever like me. I'm just too obviously a woman, whereas they'd totally like trans men.

I'M GAY, SO DO I HAVE TO DATE TRANS PEOPLE?

No, dear, you only ever have to date people you like and those you consent to have sex with.

The notion that trans people are "forcing" gay men and lesbians to date or have sex with trans people is a transphobic trope of the worst order.

DATING

Once I'd settled into my new life as Juno, I was curious to see if there was still romance out there for me. Turns out there absolutely was, but I had a lot to learn about dating as a trans person.

- People are *aware* of trans people. Through the media, real life, and the internet, we are no longer a big secret. People probably already know where they stand on potentially dating a trans person.
- Some people just haven't given it a lot of thought. A lot of people have never even met a trans person in real life! When they do, they don't instantly reject the idea of dating us. Why would they?
- No trans person is out to "trick" people into sex. We really don't need to go to the effort when there are so many willing volunteers.
- Some people are actively looking to date trans people because we are their "type." That's cool, but beware of being too objectified.
- Your safety is more important than anything. You may need to "vet" potential dates.

HOW TO MEET PEOPLE

Unless you're Rapunzel, you'll meet people every time you leave the house. It's wrong to assume everyone in the world is horrified and repulsed by trans people. Sure, a lot of folks are still waking up to our presence in the world, but most are fairly ambivalent.

I want you to hear this:

YOU ARE LOVABLE.

Very few sources are telling you that, but it's true. Our bodies are vessels for great love, support, humor, warmth, and compassion. It is *those* things people fall in love with, not some squishy bits between your legs.

So in terms of meeting partners, you can meet people in all the same places that cis and straight people meet them: in real life or online.

I've been out as trans for eight years, on hormones for six, and I've been in a relationship with my boyfriend for nearly four and a half years. It's actually the longest relationship I've ever had, and love, commitment, and companionship have all been possible.

During the first couple of years of my transition, I didn't think a relationship like this could be possible. I was only meeting people (predominately white cis men) who'd see me as an erotic experience.

This wreaked havoc on my mental health and lowered my sense of worth. I began to feel that I couldn't be loved or expect the relationship I wanted—but these men simply weren't available, and I transferred their shame on to myself.

After initially messaging my current boyfriend through a trans-friendly website, he eventually returned my message a year later when he was single. Hastily, we made up for lost time, and within the week, we'd been on several dates. To be honest, after our first date, I knew. I knew that we'd be together for the long term because we were compatible on many levels. Yes, initially my trans identity was attractive to him, but our mutual love is much deeper than that: we clicked. As the relationship unfolds, we continue to discover more about ourselves and each other. It's not always easy, but healthy relationships are available to trans people—if you want them.

Rhyannon Styles, author and artist

REAL LIFE

Like anyone, you will interact with strangers, work colleagues, and friends every day. Sometimes these relationships convert into love matches. It's really all about eye contact and confidence. No, really. My dear friend Louis has literally charmed passing cyclists off their bikes with only the power of his sultry gaze.

This is **FLIRTING**. It's ephemeral and hard to character-ize, but I do think it takes two to tango. I think you can sense when you're entering into the human mating dance, and you'd feel very silly doing it by yourself. Really, it's about gesturing your intentions to a partner.

You offer something—a compliment or kind word— and if they offer something back—a lingering glance, the touch of a hand on your arm—you carry on in that pattern.

In terms of confidence, there's only so long you can bat your eyelashes until someone really has to stick their head above the parapet and make a move.

First of all, what is it you want from this person you're attracted to? Do you want a kiss? A date? A monog-amous partnership? Is it just as simple as "I really like you"? When you know, it becomes that much easier to ask them if they want that too.

Some nifty openers:

I really like you and think we could be more than friends.

Would you like to go with me to the movies?

I have two tickets to a thing. Would you like to go?

I'd like to get to know you better.

Can we get a coffee sometime?

Are you going to so-and-so's party? Maybe we could go together?

REJECTION

You'll notice that most of those are quite closed questions. They are helpful for gauging if the other person feels the same way that you do. Sooner or later, even supermodels will have to deal with a little bit of rejection.

It happens to the best of us, and it sucks. It hurts—a lot! I really think handling rejection should be part of every school's curriculum. At the end of the day, no one is *obligated* to like you, I'm afraid, regardless of your gender and/or sexuality. I mean, they *might* change their mind over time, but you should probably just give it up as a bad job and move on.

That's not to say you should cut that person out of your life. Just because they aren't interested in exploring romantic options with you doesn't mean they won't be an amazing friend or even sexual partner. Sometimes the trick to relationships is to stop judging them against the standard that you've seen in YA novels and romance movies.* Real love and real life are a lot more complicated.

Being rejected by someone you like really hurts because it bruises your ego, and it's hard not to take it personally. Like, what's wrong with me? Answer: **NOTHING**. They just don't feel the same way you do. It is as simple as that.

There are plenty more fish in the sea. Don't lose hope.

---

* Sorry about that, btw.

ONLINE DATING

In the modern world, we don't like waiting. If you want something, Amazon Prime will put it in your mailbox within twenty-four hours. We expect nothing less when it comes to love.

Unwilling to wait for a partner to drift into our public life, we now take the hunt online. We throw our metaphorical fishing line into what is, frankly, the cesspool of the internet.

Oh, it's not all bad! I met my current partner online, and I'm very happy indeed, but I should also say I hooked an awful lot of frogs before I got a prince. For one thing, online dating via apps or websites just sucks up so much *time*. Trawling and swiping through a billion dating profiles can almost become a part-time job.

However, the **BIG PLUS** to online dating for trans and nonbinary people is that it gives you the opportunity to explain your gender to potential partners. Disclosing your gender history can be awkward, and it's another thing that cis people just don't usually have to do. IRL, if you're vibing with someone who might not be aware of your past, it's about finding that time and place to be up front. At the end of the day, *anyone* who dates has to be honest about themselves: their hopes for the future, their politics, their likes and dislikes. No relationship can be built on a foundation of fibs and lies. We *all* have to be honest when it comes to love.

If someone can't handle the fact that you're trans and/ or nonbinary, well, I guess it's good you figured that out sooner rather than later.

AN INTERLUDE ON "TRAPS"

This is a particularly spiteful way to describe trans people—usually trans women—who "pass" so well they could theoretically trick a heterosexual man into having sex with them. The word became popular via memes on the likes of the loathsome 4chan website.

I mean, this would be hilarious if it weren't literally used as justification for the murder of trans women, especially trans sex workers.

This is the reason why no trans person I have ever met would deliberately mislead sexual partners about their gender. No one is looking to get murdered.

Back to online dating. First things first: pretty much all the dating apps I know of insist on users being over eighteen, but that doesn't stop younger people from naughtily signing up. Anyway, you don't need to be over eighteen on social media apps such as Instagram, where a lot of introductions also take place in the old direct messages.

AN INTERLUDE ON NUDES— AN INTERNUDE, IF YOU PLEASE

If you're under eighteen, don't send nudes. You're distributing child pornography. Don't ask for nudes from anyone under eighteen either. That's possessing child pornography. You could find yourself in a ton of trouble. If you've seen Euphoria, that fate befalls poor trans teen Jules.

You don't have to advertise the fact that you're trans or nonbinary on social media, but if a conversation online does turn flirty, I think honesty is the best policy. If someone rejects you just for being trans, it was never going to work in the long run, and to be honest, they sound like a bit of a weenie. You've probably saved yourself some time and heartache.

You can improve your chances of success at online dating by adding details about yourself. Sell yourself! What are your interests? What are you looking for? All these details help potential dates figure out if they want to learn more. No one ever looks at a lone thirsty selfie and thinks, *Gosh, I wonder if they're funny.*

AN INTERLUDE ON "CHASERS"

Another not very nice term for someone (usually a cisgender man) who actively seeks out trans (usually) women for dating. The way I see it, a lot of women like tall men, but no one calls them "tall chasers." A lot of men like big boobs, but they don't get called names either.

Some people like trans people. Cool.

However, the discerning trans person should be mindful of what it is a new partner is looking for—is it just sex? That's fine as long as everyone is up front about things. But no one wants to be objectified or fetishized. It's no fun if someone wants to date you just because you're trans. You want someone to date you because you're smart, funny, and have similar interests.

Once you've connected with someone on the internet, it becomes about flirting once more and seeing if you want to take the step to meet in the real world.

DATING SAFELY

You don't need me to tell you that trans people are vulnerable. We've talked about the statistics. But that doesn't mean we can't enjoy dating, just that we should be wary and cautious. Nothing is more important than our continued fabulousness.

It's depressing, but because society still judges cis people who date trans people, some people try to sneak around with us on the DL. Worse, some of these people aren't strictly (or in any way) single. That's why I said you might need to do a little more vetting than a cis person might have to.

With that in mind, here are some tips for dating safely:

- Reverse image search: before meeting someone off the internet, ask to see *multiple* pictures of your date, and run a reverse image search to see if you're being catfished. Does the name they've given you match the one on the internet?
- Never give out your address until you know them a little bit.
- When meeting for the first time, choose a brightly lit public place.
- Always tell a friend where you're going and with whom.
- If something doesn't feel right on your date, you can text a chum to come meet you or ask the staff in the coffee shop or bar for assistance.
- It's Stranger Danger 101, but don't get in someone's car if you don't know them. Be similarly wary of hotel rooms or going to someone's home.

Those tips are great practice for *anyone* dating, cis or trans. We clearly have some work to do as a society to remove the stigma around dating trans people so we don't have to take on the additional security labor. If cis men weren't worried about having their masculinity challenged, they'd feel confident to express their desires and date trans women more openly.

Hello! My name is Max. By the time you're reading this, I will have married Juno. The funny thing is, if she divorces me, this will all have to be changed. I met Juno through [the dating app] Tinder. I had been on Tinder a while, and it may just be my experience, but to me it seemed like Tinder was a hellish nightmarescape of endless selfies and painful small talk.

The first thing I felt when I came across Juno's profile was how relieved I was that someone had a few lines in their "About Me" section. She immediately came across as confident, funny, and smart. She also mentioned she was trans in her profile, so I knew exactly what I was getting into. I, of course, knew about the existence of trans people but hadn't expected to match with one on Tinder. But she seemed like someone I could have an actual conversation with, so I thought, *What the heck?*

We arranged to meet up for a drink and really hit it off. Not once have I ever felt ashamed or emasculated for being lucky enough to date such a wonderful woman. My family and friends have been really supportive, but to be honest, what's the big deal?

Once again, we are getting married. Please send gifts.

Max Gallant, my husband (probably)

MAKING A RELATIONSHIP WORK

Whether you're cis or trans, making a relationship work is, well, hard work. In the first instance, it's about finding someone you're totally comfortable with, someone you can really be yourself around. When you're trans, "being yourself" takes considerably more work than it does for some. What's more, nothing in the media or culture is telling us we're desirable or loveable. For the longest time, being trans was something shameful that needed to be concealed or hidden. You can see, therefore, why "being comfortable in your skin" is a stretch to achieve on your own, never mind around someone else.

The fact is that being trans or nonbinary is going to underpin every area of your life. There's no getting away from it. When you start a relationship, it's important to find someone who understands the—and I don't use this word lightly—trauma of growing up trans in a cisgender world.

That's why some trans people like to date other trans people. I suppose it saves a lot of time in explaining your history.

When I began my transition some eleven years ago, one of my biggest fears was that I would never date again, a fear that had already delayed the process for several years. The media so often paints us as ugly or undeserving of love, and the thought of ending up alone terrified me. The reality was that dating as a trans person was hard, but from what I see of my cisgender friends, that's very much a universal struggle! I dated pre- and post-transition, meeting some lovely people along the way, but it was only when I looked within our own community that I found someone with whom I truly clicked.

Meeting Hannah four years ago was serendipitous: she had just been outed on the front page of the *Sun* newspaper, I had just appeared in *The Danish Girl*, and she popped up on my "people you may know" list on Facebook. A friend request became awkward flirtatious messages, quickly leading to the suggestion of meeting for a drink. Hannah was keen to start dating, as she had never felt comfortable doing so pretransition, and I was curious to see if dating another trans person might be the way to go.

I met Hannah under the clock at Waterloo station in December 2015, and we instantly clicked. For the first time, there were no awkward explanations about coming out, hormones, surgeries, or dysphoria, merely an unspoken understanding that allowed us to focus on those things that truly matter: what made us laugh, what music we liked, our dreams and ambitions. That first date lasted eleven hours, and we followed up with our second date the very next evening. Since then, we haven't looked back, and together we travel, make films, and speak across the world about our shared experiences as a trans couple. Against the odds, we had a baby in spring 2020.

Hannah and I are not together because we're both transgender and would never say that trans people should only date other trans people, but we would be lying if we said that hadn't made our relationship easier. Of course we argue, we're both fiery and stubborn, and we disagree over many things, as people do, but we realize how lucky we are to have found the understanding that so many appear to crave. We receive hundreds of messages every month from trans folk across the world, some of whom have been single for several years, asking how we found each other and hoping that "their person" is out there too.

I wake up every day hugely aware of how lucky I am to have found a woman like Hannah, occasionally wondering whether we would even have met had we not been part of the trans community. We'll never know the answer to that, but what I do know is that

I've found someone who accepts me for all that I am, puts up with me no matter what, doesn't take (too much of!) my nonsense, and loves me, trans or otherwise. And that is worth holding on to, no matter what.

Jake Graf, director and actor

Be reassured by the fact that many, many, many trans people are in relationships all around the world. If you want one, you can find one. It might take some time and patience, but that's true for everyone.

The big twist is that dating a trans person is very like dating *anyone*. Yes, trans people have specific trans-adjacent anxieties, but who doesn't have anxieties? It's all about compromise: What are you going to watch on Netflix? What if they're doing better than you in school? What kind of takeout should you get? What'll happen if you go to different colleges? Being in a relationship is very much a skill—another one they don't teach in schools.

HOW HEALTHY IS YOUR RELATIONSHIP?

Take the quiz! Check off any of the behaviors you observe in your relationship from yourself or your partner.

Checking messages or emails.	Demanding to know whereabouts.	Being overly critical/using putdowns in front of friends.	Being passive-aggressive: "I'm FINE," etc.
Having unfounded jealousy or suspicion.	Trying to isolate their partner from friends or family.	Using manipulation, e.g., "You'd do it if you loved me."	Encouraging their partner to fail so they become more dependent.
Having volatile mood swings.	Pressuring the other to do things they aren't comfortable with.	Blaming the other for their faults.	Acting differently with their partner than in front of their partner's friends.
Physically or verbally abusive.	Calling their partner "crazy" or attempting to gaslight them.	"Tiptoeing" around their partner for fear of upsetting them.	Dismissing their partner's emotions.

If you find yourself checking more than about three of those boxes, it might be time for a think. Difficult, though, when, on a bad day, we might all be prone to some of those behaviors.

What I want to see is better education and more mindfulness. Relationships change over time, and no one must ever be scared to walk away from one that simply isn't working. The end goal is not to be in a relationship regardless of its cost on your mental or physical health. The end goal is for you to reach something like **CONTENTMENT**, and that might only come through being single or in a different relationship.

That being said, a good relationship can be rewarding, comforting, uplifting, and—above all else—super good fun. It's like having an amazing friend that you might also **HAVE SEX WITH**, and that leads us very nicely to the next chapter.

TRANSGENDER HALL OF FAME

MUNROE BERGDORF

UK · THE MODEL ROLE MODEL

"Each of us is fighting a battle—with ourselves—all the time: 'Do I look feminine enough?', 'Am I going to be laughed at when I'm picking out cheese in Tesco?' We don't want to fight with anyone else. We're just trying to get on with our lives."

Model, DJ, and TV host Munroe Bergdorf is an outspoken advocate for LGBTQ+ rights and women of color. Often criticized in the press and online for honestly sharing her experiences, Bergdorf's journey in the media has often highlighted racism and transphobia within the beauty industry.

11

SEXYFUNTIMES

When I go back and reread *This Book Is Gay*, I'm ashamed to say that the first edition was disappointingly binary and very much geared toward cis gay men and cis lesbians. That's a big reason why I wanted to write this follow-up *and* why we updated the original last year.

We know that school sex education classes are pretty basic for most LGBTQ+ people. Too much of what you're taught in schools focuses on pregnancy prevention and STI avoidance. Both of these things are hugely important, obviously, but they shouldn't be the be-all and end-all.

In this chapter, let's explore how trans and/or nonbinary people can have a fulfilling sex life, should they want one.

That last bit is important. No one *has* to have sex if they don't want to. How do you know if you want to have sex? I think the trick is in not overthinking it. Wanting sex is a bit like wanting food: if your body wants it, it'll let you know. It's a funny, fuzzy feeling somewhere in your downstairs region.

It really is that simple. It's a hormonal thing—a dizzy cocktail of hormones in fact—and that's very relevant to trans people, because we might be in the throes of hormone replacement therapy.

Both testosterone and estrogen play a role. Estrogen makes a person receptive to the idea of sex, but testosterone is responsible for "the horn" or wanting to initiate sex. Trans women and/or nonbinary people receiving androgen blockers will traditionally find they have less interest in sex than they did before treatment, but of course this varies from person to person. Conversely, trans men and/or nonbinary people on testosterone may find themselves more horny than ever before.

That's the myth, but I think the reality is much more complicated and nuanced. My sex drive is certainly higher now, but I've been on T for years, and I feel more confident in my sexuality.

If anything, my sex drive dropped when I first started, which was probably, in part, to do with my mental health at the time. I think after a while, it picked up, and then I did become more horny. I would have to leave work early to get home for a wank!

Rory Finn, sailor

CONSENT

In most of the United States and Canada, the age of consent is **SIXTEEN**. This means people below that age cannot legally consent to a sexual relationship, even if you personally think you are ready. This is put in place to protect you from exploitation.

For people over sixteen, **CONSENT IS EVERYTHING**. I'm a big fan of ecstatic consent. You only have the sex you want, and you only get the sex you're given.

Consent is not a gray area. If both parties aren't fully invested, it's a no-no.

NO MEANS NO.

One person being too drunk to consent means no.

One person being asleep means no.

Having to coerce or pester a person into sex is a no.

Really, only a gleeful **YES!** means yes.

THE BITS THAT FEEL NICE

In this book, we don't refer to "boy's bodies" or "girl's bodies." That's reductive AF. Instead, what I'll do is run you through all the different parts of the body that **FEEL NICE**. Really, that's what sex is all about.

It's doing a bunch of things with your partner that make you feel good.

For some, the end goal is to achieve an **ORGASM**—an explosive sexual release where the whole body shakes with pleasure. Orgasms are good, but not the be-all and end-all. Sex, if done properly, should feel really good whether you achieve orgasm or not.

Let's go head to toe.

LIPS

Being a great kisser is such a skill to possess. It's really about being neither too soft nor too aggressive, but different times call for different kisses, so pay attention to what your partner likes.

TONGUE

Ah, the old French kiss! Some people like a *bit* of tongue, others less so. It really should be a bit of tongue. I'm not sure anyone likes having an entire tongue halfway down their esophagus. You'll just have to see what they do or ask.

EARLOBE

Some people find having their earlobe kissed or gently nibbled a huge turn-on.

NECK

Kissing the neck can feel lovely and tingly too.

NIPPLES

The nips are super sensitive and respond to being gently played with. Some people like them to be *less* gently played with, but you'll have to ask to find out.

BREASTS

Boobs are sensitive too, but bear in mind that the chest region might be the source of discomfort or dysphoria for some people. Check what's okay.

GENITALS

Nowhere is more sensitive than the penis or clitoris, but again, be very aware that some people have a deeply strange relationship with their front bits, regardless of how tingly they can feel. No two trans people are the same, so all you can do is talk it through with your partner and find out what they or you are comfortable with. Some people enjoy being kissed, sucked, or licked on their genitals (**ORAL SEX, GOING DOWN,** or **BLOW JOB**). Some people enjoy penetration (**SEXUAL INTERCOURSE, SHAG, SCREW**). Trans women's vaginas do not self-lubricate in the way that a cis woman's vagina would, so you'll need **LUBRICANT** if you're planning to enter one. You can get free lubricant from sexual health clinics or buy it online. Liquid Silk is the best.* You're welcome.

BUM

Some people have a prostate gland up their bum that feels nice when "massaged," which really means rubbed, I guess. People without prostates sometimes like having the bum area played with too because the anus has extrasensitive nerve endings. You know what I'm going to say...you'll have to ask. As a helpful pointer, you'll also *definitely* need lube if you're planning to put anything in a bum. Some people like penetration in the bum (**ANAL SEX**).

To douche or not to douche? That is the question Shakespeare was afraid to ask. When contemplating anal sex, some people **DOUCHE,** or squirt a bit of water into their back passage so that sneaky poo nugs don't get in the way

---

* Assuming you're not allergic to certain parabens. Sensitive lubes are available too.

of sexyfuntime. However, for various health reasons, it's not actually recommended. A jolly good wash will suffice.

FEET

Some people really like having their feet or toes played with too.

Essentially, the whole body is one big erogenous zone! Everything feels nice if you're up for it and in the mood!

You'll note that the recurring theme is **COMMUNICATION**. While no one wants to attend a sexual planning meeting, a sure sign of a healthy relationship is being able to talk, without shame or judgment, about what it is you like (or don't like) sexually. This is important for all couples, but even more so if one or both of you are trans and/or nonbinary. Do you find any words or phrases especially triggering? Do you want the lights off or a T-shirt on? Is there anything that's strictly off-limits? Deciding these things up front means the fun stuff will remain wholly fun!

Centuries of religious shaming of sex and sexuality have left us believing sex is "dirty" or "naughty." It is neither of those things. Sure, it's not for everyone, but sex is just one more thing our amazing human bodies are capable of. There is absolutely nothing "rude" when it comes to talking about sex. In fact, it's a must. Even if you think you're asexual or aromantic, there's no shame in openly discussing *your* sexuality too.

TOYS

A trans man once told me his utterly perfect response to the question "Do you have a penis?" It was, "Yes, I have a whole drawer full."

Trans people are pretty used to our bodies being a bit of a letdown at times, but that doesn't matter because, since the dawn of humanity, we have used sex aids or **SEX TOYS**. It's true! German archaeologists found what they believe is the earliest known dildo from twenty-eight thousand years ago.

The days of coyly hiding a sex toy in a box in a safe at the bottom of the ocean are long gone. You can buy sex toys online or in some stores, and they come in all shapes and sizes. Some of them vibrate, and some of them don't. Some of them are worn in a strap or harness; others are hand-held. They're all designed with the sole purpose of getting you closer to orgasm, regardless of your body type.

BE SAFE!

When you're ready—if you're ready—sex can be ace, but be mindful that **SEXUALLY TRANSMITTED INFECTIONS** (STIs) aren't going to swerve you just because you're transgender. STIs are diseases that are passed from person to person during sexual contact, either through bodily fluids or close proximity. The best way to protect against STIs is to use a condom when you have vaginal or anal sex. A condom will protect you from infections such as chlamydia, gonorrhea, herpes, syphilis, and HIV.

As trans women are thought to be particularly at risk of becoming HIV positive, you may (if you're over sixteen) also be able to access PrEP (that's pre-exposure prophylaxis), which—if taken properly—can prevent a person becoming infected. There's also PEP (post-exposure prophylaxis) for when you think you've been exposed to the HIV virus. This treatment is effective if taken within a seventy-two hour window after sex. Both PrEP and PEP can be accessed through sexual health clinics.

Remember, if your HIV-positive partner is taking their medication and the virus is "undetectable" in their system, the virus cannot be transmitted.

People with ovaries and uteruses of course run the risk of becoming **PREGNANT** too. If a sperm meets an egg, there's a potential baby situation. To avoid unwanted pregnancies, the most reliable form of birth control is the good old condom.

Of course, some trans and/or nonbinary people actively want to start a family, and that's what we'll discuss next.

TRANSGENDER HALL OF FAME

ASIA KATE DILLON

USA · THE NONBINARY BREAKTHROUGH

"As someone who is nonbinary gender identifying, I feel a particular responsibility to portray members of my community onstage and onscreen, not only as fully fleshed-out characters who are integral to the plot but as characters whose gender identity is just one of many parts that make up the whole person."

Dillon's role in the TV show *Billions* was groundbreaking in that they were (probably) the first nonbinary actor to play a nonbinary character. They raised further awareness when MTV combined its Best Actor and Actress award categories to accommodate nonbinary performers.

12

VERY GROWN-UP THINGS

When you're in the eye of the transition storm, it can be hard to see a future past the immediate burning goals: changing your name, getting the blockers, getting the hormones, getting a passport. Everything feels like *surviving*.

But then everything settles. Trust me. It's all a passing storm.

The whole idea of transitioning into your most authentic form is that you then get to live when the rain stops.

If you opt to go down the medical route, the physical changes brought on by hormones will calm down after the first three or four years. You'll always be trans, obviously, but you really do have the rest of your life to live.

For some trans people, that involves creating a family of their own.

In 2018, Jake and Hannah Graf—whom we met in

chapter 10—made the headlines as a trans couple who got married in a lavish and beautiful ceremony in London. In 2020, they welcomed a baby to their family with the help of a surrogate.

Trans and/or nonbinary people are allowed all the same things that cis people get. That's the goal of equality.

BÉBÉS

For those of us who remember the eighties and nineties, gay and lesbian parenting was wildly contentious. I remember it being debated on television shows. People said to a gay couple, "Won't your children get picked on? Don't they deserve to have a mother and a father?" Nowadays, those views feel hilariously outdated—though I have no doubt some backward Bettys still think those things.

There is no reason on earth why trans parents can't have children, although legally, we're a long way off from having systems that support us, as we'll discover in the next chapter.

Human bodies, transgender or cisgender, are usually equipped to reproduce. This biological fact is hugely important politically, because all around the world, reproductive rights are under threat. Gynecological health care is often pretty poor too. It's almost like the patriarchy deemed the bodies of cisgender men to be paramount or something.

But remember: trans bodies are often just as able to make babies as cis ones under the right conditions. However, hormone therapy does affect **FERTILITY**. It's important you're aware of that if making babies is something that interests you. Before starting HRT, doctors may well ask if you want to preserve your eggs or semen for use at a later date. Sometimes there may be additional costs for this procedure.

You may have read sensational headlines about pregnant men—dating back to the pregnancy of Thomas Beatie in 2008—but really, what's the problem? If a couple want a family and the body is able to make a baby, then why not? In Beatie's case, his wife was infertile, so they made the decision that he would carry the babies. Sometimes, being trans is a gift.

WILL'S STORY

Will and his family are somewhat unique in that Will is trans and so is his daughter.

When Juno asked me to write about what it's like raising a trans kid and being trans myself, my initial delight and excitement was quickly followed by a gray cloud of fear. I mean, what is there to say? "Hi, my name's William. I'm stepdad to three amazing kids, one of whom happens to be trans. The end." Wow, Juno's readers are going to go wild for this, I thought.

Or perhaps that's the point. I mean, there are so many barriers out there for trans folk preventing us from leading a "normal" life. Please don't crucify me for saying normal. I have no idea what it means. I mean, what is normal? Anyway, maybe living an average (a.k.a. boring) kind of life as a trans guy with a kind of "regular" family is what some people want, or need, to hear about.

So here goes.

I've always wanted a family, to be a dad, but that was confusing for me growing up. I wanted a family, but there was no way on this earth I was ever going to give birth. Though I was assigned female at birth, it just wasn't for me. I couldn't imagine it, ever. The thought of it just felt wrong (props to the trans guys who do, btw). I couldn't see a way forward.

Fast-forward too many years to count, and I met my (now) fiancée Ella. We've been together for thirteen years. She had three kids from her previous relationship when we met, and they were all very young; the youngest was only three months old. We hit it off instantly, and although I was a bit overwhelmed by the prospect of going from zero to three kids at breakneck speed, we decided to give it a go. So here we are. I didn't go out with the intention of finding a "ready-made family." It just kind of happened.

I transitioned during my relationship with Ella, after a particularly difficult few years following the realization that our youngest might be trans. To be honest, I hadn't even heard of the term *transgender* until we went to the doctor. This had a massive impact on me at the time, as I had always felt sorry for her wanting to be a girl and really empathized with how she felt but from the opposite perspective.

With the help and support from the consultants at the gender clinic in London, we supported her social transition to become Jessica, and she and we, as a family, were much happier.

Learning that there was something that described how I'd felt all my life was probably the most profound experience I've ever had. I'll never forget that feeling of "That's me!" when hearing about and researching trans issues for the first time. Those early years of it all seeming very scary and daunting, telling our friends and family about Jessica, and then coming out myself a few years later, feels like a lifetime ago—almost.

I would be lying if I said life with a trans child was easy, but I don't see it as different from any other child who has particular needs—our eldest has autism, for example. There are specialist appointments to attend at the gender clinic for monitoring, regular trips to the doctor for blockers, and general stuff like keeping an eye out for bullying. I guess we're just used to the day-to-day living side of things; it's our "normal." We are probably more vigilant than the average family, certainly more aware of "safe" LGBTQ+ places to visit on days out or holidays. We consider single-sex spaces like changing rooms before attending swimming pools or the beach, for example. We try to make sure that the kids can change safely without running into issues from people who may be ignorant or are just downright bigoted. It affects us all really, but it certainly doesn't stop us going out and enjoying life.

On balance, despite the difficulties, I wouldn't change a thing. I feel privileged to be part of an amazing and supportive community. I feel like my eyes have been opened to a whole world of happiness and authenticity. I've met some of the most incredible people, some of whom have had a really tough time, but they are now the inspirational role models of modern times.

Life as a trans or rainbow family, as we call it, is great. We are kind, caring, loving, and supportive to each other. We try to spread this kindness to the wider community we live in. We're very mindful that life isn't always as straightforward for everyone, and you have no idea what people around you are going through, so just be kind.

I've never felt restricted in what I can or can't do as a trans person, and that includes having a family. I may not have known how I was going to achieve it or if I ever would, but I just went with the flow of life and love, and everything fell into place. I feel very lucky to be where I am today.

WILL, diversity consultant

THE FAMILY YOU FIND

Family doesn't always look like a child's drawing of one: a mommy and daddy standing next to a square house with a white picket fence.

As we all have different relationships with the families we were born into, it's no great surprise that a lot of queer people formulate their own "found families" as popularized in Armistead Maupin's classic *Tales of the City* series. In those books and TV shows, a diverse group of LGBTQ+ people live with a kindly trans woman called Anna Madrigal. The same is true of the more recent series *Pose*, in which transgender ballroom "mothers" look after families of queer "children."

It's *so* important to make trans friends, either in real

life or online. Cis allies are amazing, but other trans and/or nonbinary people understand what it is we've been through. It can be a strange experience, and it's so much easier if you don't have to explain all the hurdles and hardships every time you want to vent.

I reached out to trans people who inspired me, and I'm very lucky that I now consider some incredible figures to be dear friends. One of those is Mzz Kimberley, one of London's most recognizable figures.

I grew up a very sad child in Michigan, always hiding who I was, not accepting who I was, living with a family who didn't understand me, and hating myself. In New York, I could be free. Finding friends who understood me helped me through the beginning of my journey. In NY, I met fabulous people, but there was still a small part of me that hid because I hadn't come to terms with my true self.

After three years living in NY, I made my way to London and met my first best friend who was a trans woman, Zsarday Forde, known as the "Skinny Bitch." Usually you meet your best friend as a kid. Meeting Zsarday was a breath of fresh air. She was kind and really understood the woman in me. With Zsarday, I felt safe, and together we experienced and learned what life had to offer. Having that support helped me develop and start to accept living my truth. Having someone to speak to about your true feelings is powerful.

Sadly, I lost Zsarday over ten years ago, but I learned how important community is. Being able to support members of your community and have them support you is the only way to evolve with your true emotions. Living your truth is easier in today's climate, but supporting members of your own community can make a huge difference in your life. Having someone from your community who can truly understand your experiences with sex, medical transition, wigs, clothes, etc. could save your life. Your cis friends will support you but never truly understand those deep-rooted feelings. Being supported by the gender clinic, which is cis-led, helped in many ways, but I learned more about my transitioning from my community. Today the trans community are fortunate to have cliniQ, a trans-led well-being and health service.

I started "Mzz Kimberley's LIFE" in 2019 because I wanted to give my community a platform to feel empowered, come together, get to know each other, and show the world that we are decent human beings with feelings and love in our hearts. We did our first trans-led fashion show with models and performers in city hall, which was groundbreaking. The show was a heavily diverse cast.

Having different cultural backgrounds, including the disabled trans community, was important because everyone deserves to shine.

Getting to know more about different cultures in our community is powerful, because your support network grows even further. When we truly come together and support each other, we will be able to evolve even more in society.

Mzz Kimberley, a.k.a. Kim Tatum, actress and cabaret singer, founding director of LIFE, patron of cliniQ, ParaPride, and AIDS Memorial UK

TRANSGENDER HALL OF FAME

KYE ALLUMS

USA · THE ACTIVIST ATHLETE

"I have been traveling to high schools sharing my story, educating people on being trans, starting conversations that nobody wants to talk about. I'm just trying to show people that it is possible to play with a trans person on your team, it is possible to have a trans student; you teach them like anyone else. I've found that people want to learn and that just because someone is ignorant doesn't mean that they will never understand."

Kye Allums was (probably) the first openly transgender man to play basketball in the official college division. Since retiring from competition, he has devoted his life to activism and founded the I Am Enough project for LGBTQ+ youth.

13

YOU AND THE LAW

You know you're in a minority group when, all of a sudden, you realize your life is way more political than most people's. If you identify as transgender, nonbinary, genderqueer, or gender nonconforming, there are people in positions of power debating your rights. It's exhausting and troubling. No one likes living on thin ice.

It's angering to have your life used as a political bargaining chip. With the rise in trans awareness (broadly a good thing) came a rise in moral panic (a wholly bad thing). Although trans people have been pottering along in society for decades, centuries even, many people thought this was all very new and trendy and we had to have a national conversation at once.

This "debate" was seized on by the right-wing media. They couldn't very well scrutinize the failings of our right-wing leaders, could they? That would be much too honest. And so Muslims, migrants, and transgender people became daily distractions to fill tabloid space.

As such, it's really important for you to know where you stand with the law. As ever, I'll try and keep this as simple and jargon-free as possible.

U.S. LEGAL RIGHTS

The situation in the United States is vastly complicated by the fact that each jurisdiction or state has very different rules. In some ways, the States are behind the UK with no federal (i.e., nationwide) laws protecting transgender people's rights, but at a state level, some states have laws that exceed those in the UK. It really does depend on where you live, which is bad news if you're a minor and can't yet move.

Some states allow for the gender marker "X" on drivers' licenses, such as Arkansas, California, Colorado, Maine, Maryland, Massachusetts, Minnesota, Nevada, New Jersey, New York, Oregon, Pennsylvania, Utah, Vermont, Washington, and Washington, DC. In 2016, Oregon became the first state to officially recognize nonbinary identities.

CANADIAN LEGAL RIGHTS

Much like the United States, the process for legally changing your gender varies across the country. Policies for changing genders and protections from discrimination vary among the provinces and territories. However, in 2017, Bill C-16 was passed, adding "gender identity and expression" to the Canadian Human Rights Act.

THE GLOBAL SITUATION

ILGA—the International Lesbian, Gay, Bisexual, Trans, and Intersex Association—publishes detailed guidance about the ever-shifting political situation for LGBTQ+ people all around the world. Things can change so quickly that it's better for a person to keep an eye on their resources than it is for me to write a list of unsafe places that may drift in and out of accuracy.

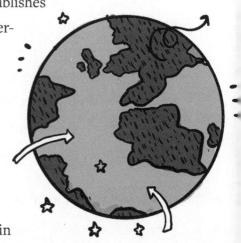

One of the problems is what constitutes "gender change." In some places, this merely involves being allowed to change your name. Some countries still insist on sterilization (preventing people from ever having kids) ahead of legal transition. There are wildly different rules for those under eighteen too.

UNITED KINGDOM

As Christine Burns touched on in chapter 3, the **GENDER RECOGNITION ACT 2004** was (at the time) a revolutionary piece of legislation. It allows a person—over the age of eighteen—to legally change sex and acquire a new birth certificate. In the eyes of the law, you are now legally your new gender and receive a **GENDER RECOGNITION CERTIFICATE**.

Transgender people are also protected under the **EQUALITY ACT 2010**. This legislation stops people who've undergone "gender reassignment" from being discriminated against by employers, organizations, and services. This essentially means that someone can't bar you from using the correct public toilets or changing rooms. So that clears that up.

REPUBLIC OF IRELAND

People couldn't legally change their sex or gender in Ireland until 2015, but when they introduced legislation, they went way further than the UK. In Ireland, a person can legally change gender *without* the requirement of medical intervention. This change is possible through self-determination for anyone over eighteen (who is a resident in Ireland and listed on Irish registers of birth or adoption). People aged sixteen to eighteen can secure a court order to exempt them from the normal requirement to be at least eighteen. Ireland is one of several legal jurisdictions in the world where people may legally change gender through self-determination, making them a global leader in trans rights. Oh, Ireland, twelve points! *heart emoji*

AUSTRALIA

A little like the United States, the situation in Australia depends on where you are, since each territory has slightly different rules. Some areas are very progressive—even legally recognizing nonbinary identities—while others (looking at you, Queensland and New South Wales) still require gender reassignment surgeries before they'll grant formal recognition of a gender change. WTF? Get with it!

NEW ZEALAND

New Zealand is among the most progressive places in the world when it comes to transgender rights.* Remember that the indigenous Māori people had trans identities long before white invaders came. In 2012, the government simplified the process for changing one's ID. In 2018, the government lifted a cap on the number of surgeries they would fund, but since the retirement of the only NZ surgeon performing

---

* And it's where I'm heading if things get much worse in the UK.

gender reassignment surgery in 2014, there are now reports of very long delays in receiving some medical treatments. This situation will hopefully change soon.

INDIA

There have been recent laws introduced in India that, while designed to protect trans people from violence, require trans people to provide proof of gender reassignment surgeries. Obviously, this is deeply problematic, as many trans people can't access or do not want those surgeries. The laws also fail to mention protections for trans people in the workplace or in marriages.

India is in a period of change regarding all LGBTQ+ laws. Since I wrote *This Book Is Gay*, same-sex relationships were legal, then illegal, then legal again. With such rapidly changing human rights, we must all apply pressure to governments to protect their most vulnerable citizens.

TOURISM

All trans and nonbinary people should be wary of foreign travel to countries that have a history of not respecting transgender people—even those with passports or gender certificates. Sometimes these countries include those where it's legal to be transgender, but colloquially people have been challenged at customs—looking at you, United Arab Emirates.

Stay safe and be smart. Before you travel overseas, it takes little effort to google the LGBTQ+ rights of that country. Yes, it's maddening that we don't have the same freedom of movement as cisgender people, but better safe than sorry.

TRANSGENDER HALL OF FAME
CAITLYN JENNER

USA · THE REALITY ROYAL

"There's nothing more, nothing better in life than to wake
up in the morning, look at yourself in the mirror, and
feel comfortable with yourself and who you are."

An outspoken and occasionally controversial figure, it's undeniable
that Caitlyn Jenner's enormously public transition raised awareness
of trans people more than almost anyone else in history. As part of
the most famous family in reality TV, Jenner introduced people all
around the world to what it means to go through gender transition.

14
WHAT NEXT?

Today, I went to see *Frozen II* at the cinema. It's so cool to see transgender narratives done so well on the big screen, isn't it?

What? You don't believe me? Elsa realizes she's different as a child and shuts herself away from the world until she can't deny her true self any more and puts on a fancy dress. She's then welcomed back to Arendelle as her authentic self. The sequel goes even further. You see, it turns out there's more to Elsa than simply being a queen. She's actually a powerful elemental being.

And that brings me neatly to my point.

So you're trans or nonbinary or genderqueer? Great! Now, what next?

That's not supposed to be dismissive of your ordeal/journey thus far. It's just acknowledging that being trans or nonbinary is only one part of your life—yes, a big part, but one of many.

We are all big, delicious cocktails. Some ingredients are key to our identities: our gender, sexuality, race, faith, whether we perceive ourselves to have a disability, our economic background. These elements will have a huge impact on your entire life. Often, online, we refer to these things as **PRIVILEGES** or factors that influence how well we are able to steer through life. If you imagine a boat floating downstream, a canoe with less baggage is going to go faster, smoother, and easier than one with a ton of stuff.

In our patriarchal society, being trans, being from a minority ethnic background, being poor, being a woman (cis or trans), being gay or bi, or having a disability does affect how easily you are able to...well...live *comfortably*, free from prejudice, harassment, and discrimination.

The way you *look* will similarly impact your life. People are still outrageously rude toward people who are considered both overweight and underweight. People with acne or scars, red hair, or who are very tall or short may also face scrutiny.

The good news is that the first lesson you were taught in nursery school—"It's what's inside that counts"—is thankfully true. While how you look and your identity do have an impact on your life (they shouldn't, but I won't lie, they do), ultimately they are not how you will triumph.

Some random white, cisgender, straight, nondisabled

man is always quick to let you know on social media that they are suffering too.

I always say, "Of course, and I'm sorry to hear that, but you aren't suffering because you're straight, white, cisgender, and male." He isn't getting wolf whistles; he isn't being called "tr*nny" or "f*gg*t"; he can use every bathroom in every building with ease. Mental health, for instance, doesn't discriminate, but a Black trans woman has to deal with mental health issues on top of (and because of) transphobia, racism, and misogyny. I'd have thought that would be obvious.

I believe trans people develop a thick skin, an armor. How could we not? In the face of great adversity, we took hold of our lives and rewrote destiny. But then what?

What *really* matters in life is a mixture of your skills and personality. Those things are what will truly help you to succeed. So really, I've brought you as far as I can. I, along with all the other contributors in this book, have offered advice and also proved beyond any doubt that there is life beyond figuring out your gender identity.

But *look* at the contributors! Look at the Hall of Fame personalities. Yes, they are all trans and/or nonbinary, but they are also highly talented, skilled, clever, funny, kind, intelligent, and charming.

And you need that cocktail of traits. I know some phenomenally talented people—who shall remain nameless—who have self-sabotaged their careers at every turn through being disorganized, rude, or unreliable. Likewise, I know some people who perhaps aren't the most skilled but through cheerful charm and sheer work ethic have risen to the top of the pile.

It sounds bizarre, but take it from me. After a while, you get bored of talking about gender. I won't lie; I found writing some parts of this book really difficult, purely because I keep having the same conversations—about identity or defending myself against transphobia. After a while, you're like, *Won't someone just talk to me about this week's* Dancing with the Stars *result?*

I'm half kidding but half very serious. You know as well as I do that the world is a hot mess right now. Literally. If the creeping rise of fascism doesn't get you, novel coronaviruses or climate disaster will. What's the point in being your most authentic self if there isn't a planet for you to live on?

It might seem a little odd to end a book about trans identities with a stark warning about global crises, but that's my point: there's only one world, and it's **OUR WORLD TOO.**

What I hope you've learned is that there's a place for every last one of you on this planet. You don't have to apologize for taking up space. In the last twenty years, trans awareness has leaped forward like never before. There's no going back into the shadows. We are in a period of adjustment,

certainly: a lot of people, including our elected leaders, are still trying to figure out what our presence means.

Spoiler alert: it means **NOTHING**. We are **PEOPLE**.

I hope that, very soon, people realize that human lives are of equal importance. Remember, you have a voice in all this. Our leaders are only our leaders if we elect them. By registering to vote and voting, you are ensuring we choose leaders who have the interests of the LGBTQ+ community in mind.

Do not let the bastards get you down. Go out there and show the world how amazing you are.

If you've got this far, you are already amazing. Keep going.

The most defiant, most powerful thing you can do is **LIVE** and **CONTINUE TO LIVE**. Live your life openly, colorfully, and in stereo. Live with compassion, kindness, and humor.

LIVE.

TRANSGENDER HALL OF FAME

GEORGINA BEYER

NEW ZEALAND · THE POLITICAL POWERHOUSE

"People still regard the gender thing as being relatively recent in our modern history, but we've been around for millennia. Fa'afafine. Takatāpui. When you have words in ancient languages to include us, that should send a message that this didn't happen last week."

Georgina Beyer, a former sex worker, became the first ever transgender woman in the world to hold political office. First as mayor of Carterton and then as Labor MP for Wairarapa, she held office from 1999 to 2007. Beyer's story demonstrates that trans people can call the shots in society too.

PART THREE

HELP AND ADVICE

15
QUESTIONS ANSWERED

I asked my Twitter followers what they'd most like to know. Before I answer these, I'd like to repeat that there is no high council, no "powerful trans lobby." This is simply one elder, passing on some wisdom she got from her elders.

Q. DOES GENDER DYSPHORIA EVER COMPLETELY GO AWAY?

A. For me, it was certainly a very gradual process. It was a bit like moving into a new home. For a very long time, nothing was quite the way I wanted it to be. Over about four years, my life *and* my body changed, and—bit by bit—everything was the way I wanted it. That said, neither my body nor my home is ever going to be exactly how I would want it to be! In an ideal world, I'd look like Faith, the vampire slayer, in 1999 forever. But that's never going to happen. I feel less dysphoric but still occasionally dissatisfied. Who doesn't?

Q. SINCE WHEN HAVE TRANS PEOPLE BEEN AROUND?

The exact date is very hard to pin down, but as long as societies have been recorded, there is evidence of gender-nonconforming people. The term *transgender* has been in use for about fifty years. There's loads more facts and figures in chapter 3!

Q. AT WHAT MOMENT IN YOUR LIFE DID YOU KNOW IT WAS RIGHT FOR YOU TO TRANSITION?

Most of it was due to education. I was about twenty-eight when I seriously asked what transition meant and what it would mean for me personally. I schooled myself by talking to other trans people and a therapist. The decision to come out in 2013 was because I simply felt like I was wasting time and wanted as much of my life to be Junofied as possible.

Q. ASIDE FROM THE BARE MINIMUM (USING THE CORRECT PRONOUNS, ETC.), WHAT ARE SOME WAYS THAT ALLIES CAN HELP THEIR TRANS FRIENDS FEEL SEEN AND SUPPORTED?

On a personal level, *include* your friends! Tag them in your social media pictures! Invite them to things in real life! Introduce them to your cis friends! Being trans can feel quite isolating, so making them feel wanted and loved is really important. Also, offer to accompany them to places if they don't feel safe. Can you spare a taxi fare or get them an Uber?

I say this a lot too, but if you're in a financial position to, consider donating to surgery crowdfunding campaigns. There are plenty out there. Finally, support politicians with progressive agendas who are seeking to make the world more accessible for trans people.

Q. HOW DO I TRANSITION WITHOUT MY PARENTS FINDING OUT? I STILL LIVE WITH THEM, AND I KNOW MY TEACHERS/CLASSMATES ARE ACCEPTING, BUT EVERY STEP I MAKE IN THAT DIRECTION FEELS TERRIFYING.

The good news is you have your **WHOLE LIFE** to figure all this out and redefine your relationship with your parents. All in good time—nothing transition-wise ever happens very quickly. I always say don't underestimate your loved ones. They want you to be happy.

Bear in mind, everyone wears different "masks" in different groups of people. Maybe it's okay that your friends at school know you as one name and the people at home another—at least for the time being while you figure out how, if, and when you do want to include your parents in the process.

16

ADVICE FOR PARENTS AND CAREGIVERS

Hello! Thank you for reading this section. Already, that shows you're *listening*. By and large, young people need to feel listened to and validated. This chapter of the book will set out what to expect if a young person in your life is in some way gender nonconforming.

I really feel for the parents of trans people. If you're **CISGENDER** (happy with the gender you were assigned at birth), you're never going to *fully* understand **GENDER DYSPHORIA**. That's why, for so long, we relied on telling people "I was born in the wrong body"—it's the most basic shorthand there is for something incredibly complicated.

I'm happy to share that telling my mum and dad I'm trans was the hardest thing I've ever done. I had about six months of therapy in advance simply to get through it.

Young people probably aren't going to be in the position to afford that, so them coming out to you is incredibly brave, braver than you can comprehend, and a sign that they trust you with this information. So that's a good thing, right?

I am not a parent. Well, I have a chihuahua, but he is unlikely to come out as gender nonconforming, because gender is a **SOCIAL CONSTRUCT**. There is no one-size-fits-all approach to parenting a gender-nonconforming child, because no two trans people are the same. There isn't one way to be transgender. It's worth bearing in mind that every trans and/or nonbinary adult was a trans or nonbinary child.* This is not a decision or choice. We were, in the words of Lady Gaga, "born this way."

My guess is that you're reading this book because your young person has given it to you in the hope you might better understand what they're going through. It could also be that, with all the trash in the tabloids, you've started questioning if your child might be gender nonconforming in some way. Either way, I hope this book offers some hope that the sky is categorically not falling.

Of course you have questions. Who wouldn't? What I can do is tell you what questions I wish my parents had asked me.

---

* Definitions of labels like this can be found in chapter 2.

1. HOW LONG HAVE YOU FELT THIS WAY?

This will help you to ascertain if they're in a "crisis" as such. Figuring out your gender is deeply confusing and can feel like you're in the eye of the storm. You can reassure them that they have as much time as they need to get to grips with things.

The mantra for parents of trans youth has become **PERSISTENT, INSISTENT, CONSISTENT**. Are they telling you *a lot*, *quite urgently*, and has it been going on *a while*? The idea is that if a person is repeatedly and urgently giving you the same information, why would you doubt it? The problem I have with this simplistic method is that shame and embarrassment kept me quiet for the best part of thirty years. Not all young people are brave enough to say it. That said, my behavior was consistently feminine, even if I wasn't insistent about anything.

Do *not* ask about the permanence of thinking or use the dreaded "phase" word. Gender expression—the way you dress or do your hair—isn't *ever* permanent. Why would it be for trans youth?

What's important is giving them the space and time to figure things out.

2. HOW DO YOU FEEL?

Being transgender is *not* a mental illness, but living in the wrong gender is stressful, anxiety making, and sometimes miserable. Check up on your child's mental health in the same way you would their bodily health.

3. WHAT DO YOU WANT TO HAPPEN NEXT?

Gender is a big abstract concept, so focusing on something practical gives everyone a sense of control. The next step could be making an appointment at your family doctor or with a school counselor, informally changing your child's name or pronouns, or helping them to tell the rest of the family.

Reassure them again by stressing they have time. Rome wasn't built in a day. You have the rest of your life to figure out who you are—and that's true of everyone. Transition isn't and has never been a race against time.

Do *not* ask **WHY** this is happening. No trans person knows. It just is.

4. DO YOU WANT MEDICAL INTERVENTION?

This isn't a given. Not all trans people want to go down the medical route. Nothing is going to happen very quickly, so there's lots of time for everyone to talk and think.

I can see it would be tempting to "call in the doctors" to make sense of a confusing time, but understand that for those transgender people who want to explore medical options, long waiting lists can add frustration and distress to an already complicated process. Going down the medical route is a deeply frustrating time.

5. WHAT CAN I DO TO HELP?

Transgender people need to feel like they have people on their side. The path ahead will be complex and wearying at times: bureaucracy, waiting times, transphobia. No one is transitioning for *fun*; look at it that way. If there is a trans child in the family, the whole family is going on a journey together.

If your child is under eighteen, they're definitely going to need an adult champion. It is *you* who might need to talk to teachers and the doctor. It is *you* who might have to insist that friends and family use a different name. It is *you* who might be responsible for applying for a new passport or ID.

6. WHERE CAN I LEARN MORE?

Your child is not an expert. **THE TREVOR PROJECT** and **TRANS LIFELINE** and **GENDER DIVERSITY** (details in the next chapter) have a wealth of resources available online.

Do follow transgender adults on social media: we are out there living our lives. There are also online support groups for parents of trans youth. You are certainly not alone. Just think: you're now in the exact same position as Cher and Charlize Theron, so that's pretty cool.

7. WHERE'S THE HARM?

Research shows that children have a very fixed notion of their gender from as young as three years old and also that their identity exists prior to any sort of social transition.[*] An earlier study showed that validating or affirming your child's gender preferences is better for their well-being than denying them.[†]

That said, you don't need me to tell you that fighting with your child is more difficult than giving them time and space. In this case, to fundamentally deny who they are would cause huge distress. Imagine feeling like, on top of being a quirk of nature, you also have to battle your parents.

---

[*] Kristina R. Olson, Aidan C. Key, and Nicholas R. Eaton, "Gender Cognition in Transgender Children," *Psychological Science* 26, no. 4 (April 2015): 467–74, https://doi.org/10.1177/0956797614568156; Selin Gülgöz et al., "Similarity in Transgender and Cisgender Children's Gender Development," *Proceedings of the National Academy of Sciences* 116, no. 49 (December 2019): 24480–85, https://doi.org/10.1073/pnas.1909367116.

[†] Ilana Sherer, "Social Transition: Supporting Our Youngest Transgender Children," *Pediatrics* 137, no. 3 (March 2016): e20154358, https://doi.org/10.1542/peds.2015-4358.

Well, that just makes a tough situation even tougher.

It shouldn't take Sherlock Holmes to deduce that scaffolding your children makes for a happy family situation. Scaffolding is not blindly supporting every whim your child makes (yes, we all went through the "I am a cat" period, cis and trans alike). It's more about listening, learning, accepting, trusting, and believing.

Being transgender is not a mental illness. However, compared with cisgender peers, trans youth are two to three times more likely to suffer from depression, anxiety, or suicidal thoughts.[‡] Navigating a cisgender world when you're trans is really, really tough. A young trans person desperately needs you on their side.

Again, we don't know precisely why some people are transgender, but it does keep happening. For us, being trans is totally normal. It's about creating an environment where your child feels **SAFE** to tell you whatever is troubling them. If they feel they will be rejected or derided in any circumstances, how could they truly open up about their life at all? I think all parents would rather have a bond of trust with their child than not. But the trust has to be earned.

[‡] "Transgender Youth at Risk for Depression, Suicide," Harvard School of Public Health, https://www.hsph.harvard.edu/news/hsph-in-the-news/transgender-youth-at-risk-for-depression-suicide/; Daniel Shumer, "Health Disparities Facing Transgender and Gender Nonconforming Youth Are Not Inevitable," *Pediatrics* 141, no. 3 (March 1, 2018).

THE SKY IS NOT FALLING.

Immediately after I came out, I experienced a year or two of turmoil in all areas of my life. Coming out as transgender is an upheaval whatever stage of life you're at.

However, understand that eventually everything does settle down.

Crisis mode is never permanent. Whatever path a transgender person takes, there are bound to be ups and downs, but we know what we're getting into. We understand—to an extent—that the trials of transition are outweighed by the merit of being true to ourselves. Eventually, trans becomes the new normal.

After the first couple of years, my "issues" became less focused on self and body and more on career, relationships, and family: the same as any cisgender person.

Being transgender isn't always *easy*, sure, but it certainly isn't the end of the world. That's the thing with kids, isn't it? You're never quite sure what you're going to get. If you don't want an LGBTQ+ child, use a condom. The culture we live in is telling you that your child being transgender is a worst-case scenario. That's not true. It's simply a scenario.

I asked Mermaids, one of the UK's leading charities that support young trans people and their families, what advice they'd give to parents. This is what they said:

Here are five of our top tips:

1. **No one can imagine what it's like to be a child trying to find the words to tell someone that you think you might be trans.** It is an incredibly brave thing to do. Consider for one moment that the same child may have been wishing this thought away for months or even years. Imagine being this scared of your own thoughts and alone. Imagine a world where the people who love and care for you reject or ignore this cry for help. If you are ever privileged enough to have someone tell you they are trans, just remember three things: LISTEN carefully to what they are saying, remind them that you LOVE them, and REASSURE them that things will be okay (and then phone Mermaids). You do not need in-depth knowledge of what it means to be trans or gender-diverse. Everyone's transition is individual, so seek the right information as and when you need it.

2. **This is not your fault.** There is nothing you have said or done that has "made your child this way." It is who they are. It is an intrinsic part of them.

3. **Believe what they are saying to you.** Don't imagine it is a phase or that they have been watching too much YouTube. Start off with the open heart of belief, remembering that this is still the child you have loved up to now and will continue to love.

4. **Don't be afraid to ask questions.** It is better to ask than to get

it wrong. Your child would rather you ask them what they want going forward than for you to not ask at all.

5.   **Listen, believe, trust, and accept your child's words.** You are their rock, anchorage, and safety point. They can share their worries and fears with you, talk through their thoughts and feelings, and know that someone is there when/if the rest of the world isn't.

This book is just a starting point! There's loads of information out there.

17

FURTHER SUPPORT

A book or a website is no substitute for talking to real-life people. It's especially good, I think, to meet other trans, nonbinary, and gender-nonconforming people your own age. It's really good to know that you're not the only person who feels the way you do or who is going through it.

Here are some signposts to point you in the right direction.

GENDER DIVERSITY
GENDERDIVERSITY.ORG

Gender Diversity increases the awareness and understanding of the wide range of gender diversity in children, adolescents, and adults by providing family support, building community, increasing societal awareness, and improving well-being for people of all gender identities and expressions.

NATIONAL BLACK TRANS ADVOCACY COALITION
BLACKTRANS.ORG

Through the national advocacy center and affiliate state chapters, BTAC works daily, advocating to end poverty, discrimination in all forms, and human inequities faced in health, employment, housing, and education that are rooted in systemic racism to improve the lived experience of transgender people.

THE TREVOR PROJECT
THETREVORPROJECT.ORG

Founded in 1998 by the creators of the Academy Award–winning short film *Trevor*, the Trevor Project is the leading national organization providing crisis intervention and suicide prevention services to lesbian, gay, bisexual, transgender, queer, and questioning young people under twenty-five. The Trevor Project runs a twenty-four-hour helpline at 1-866-488-7386.

TRANS LIFELINE
TRANSLIFELINE.ORG

A 24/7 hotline staffed by transgender people for transgender people. Trans Lifeline is primarily for transgender people in a crisis, from struggling with gender identity to thoughts of self-harm.

United States: 1-877-565-8860; Canada: 1-877-330-6366

TRANSGENDER LAW CENTER
TRANSGENDERLAWCENTER.ORG

Grounded in legal expertise and committed to racial justice, the Transgender Law Center employs a variety of community-driven strategies to keep transgender and gender-nonconforming people alive, thriving, and fighting for liberation.

GLOBAL RESOURCES
THE ALBERT KENNEDY TRUST
WWW.AKT.ORG.UK/

AKT is an LGBTQ+ homelessness charity working with young people aged sixteen to twenty-five, with offices in London, Manchester, Bristol, and Newcastle.

London: 020 7831 6562; Manchester: 0161 228 3308; Bristol: 07761246386; Newcastle: 0191 281 0099.

CANADIAN PROFESSIONAL ASSOCIATION
FOR TRANSGENDER HEALTH
CPATH.CA

CPATH is an interdisciplinary professional organization that works to support the health, well-being, and dignity of trans and gender-diverse people. CPATH seeks to be both connected with and responsive to the needs emerging from gender-diverse and trans people and communities.

CHILDLINE

CHILDLINE.ORG.UK

Childline runs a totally free helpline (9:00 a.m. to midnight) at 0800 1111.

GENDERED INTELLIGENCE

GENDEREDINTELLIGENCE.CO.UK

Gendered Intelligence is a not-for-profit charity established in 2008. They work with the trans community and those who impact on trans lives; they particularly specialize in supporting young trans people under the age of twenty-one. They also deliver trans youth programs, support for parents and caregivers, professional development, trans awareness training for all sectors, and educational workshops for schools, colleges, universities, and other educational settings. Their mission is to increase understanding of gender diversity. Their vision is of a world where people are no longer constrained by narrow perceptions and expectations of gender and where diverse gender expressions are visible and valued.

Every year, Gendered Intelligence organizes the most fun trips away for trans youth—usually funded—so that you can hang out with other people just like you! Last year, they even took a bunch of trans kids to Trans Pride in Brighton!

ICALL
ICALLHELPLINE.ORG

iCALL is a free telephone and email-based counseling service run by the School of Human Ecology, Tata Institute of Social Sciences, India. Its team of qualified and trained mental health professionals supports anyone in emotional and psychological distress and is inclusive of gender and sexual orientation. Telephone: 915–298–7821 (Mon–Sat: 8:00 a.m. to 10:00 p.m.).

KIDS HELPLINE
KIDSHELPLINE.COM.AU

Kids Helpline is Australia's only free, private, and confidential 24/7 phone and online counseling service for young people aged five to twenty-five. Telephone: 1800 55 1800.

LGBT IRELAND
LGBT.IE

Telephone helpline and instant messaging service for all LGBTQ+ people. Also links LGBTQ+ people with more local services in their area. Telephone: 1800 929 539.

MERMAIDS
MERMAIDSUK.ORG.UK

Mermaids was established in 1995 and has since supported

countless trans, nonbinary, and gender-diverse young people across the United Kingdom. What they know from their experience is that each and every young person has a unique journey and that there is no "one way" to be gender-diverse. Nor is there any single way for a young person to find the confidence they need. However, there is one thing that can make your journey as comfortable as possible, and that's support.

Mermaids has a helpline and webchat and forum services so you can reach out and seek the support you need. Please don't hesitate to get in touch if you are gender questioning or gender diverse seeking friendship and validation. You do not need to know where you will end up, but they do want you to know that they are here.

MINUS18
MINUS18.ORG.AU

Minus18 creates fun-filled spaces where Australian LGBTQIA+ young people belong and are celebrated. Being visible, making friends, and feeling supported are what their events are about.

OUTLINE
OUTLINE.ORG.NZ

OutLine's trained volunteers welcome calls from people in

New Zealand to discuss topics around sexual orientation, gender identity, and diverse sex characteristics. They can help you find sources of trusted information, connection to community or peers, and medical or mental health services that welcome LGBTQ+ people. Telephone: 0800 688 5463 (6:00 p.m. to 9:00 p.m.)

TRANSLATIN@ COALITION
TRANSLATINACOALITION.ORG

Members of the TransLatin@ Coalition are transgender Latina leaders who come together from all across the country, donating their time to organize and advocate for the issues and needs of the trans Latin@ community living in the United States.

RAINBOWYOUTH
RY.ORG.NZ

RainbowYOUTH works with young people, their families, and their wider communities in New Zealand to connect them with accurate and correct information and services that will provide safe and respectful support. They also offer one-to-one support sessions.

SWITCHBOARD LGBT
SWITCHBOARD.LGBT

Switchboard LGBT is a nationwide listening service for all LGBTQ+ people that can be reached between 10:00 a.m. and 10:00 p.m. at 0300 330 0630.

QTOPIA
QTOPIA.ORG.NZ

Qtopia provides support for rainbow young people in Christchurch and South Island, New Zealand. They can connect you with their youth groups, family support, and resources, including funding for counseling services.

YAARIYAN
HUMSAFAR.ORG/YAARIYAN/

Yaariyan (Friendship) is a voluntary LGBTQ+ youth initiative and support group run by the Humsafar Trust in India. It has an online forum, organizes offline events, and facilitates youth access to health and social supports.

LOCAL GROUPS

Wherever you are in the world, there's probably a support group near you—even in countries with questionable laws regarding LGBTQ+ people. There's way too many to list here, but if you contact the national services I've listed, they may well be able to put you in touch with a local group.

Many areas have youth groups specifically for LGBTQ+ people, and I can't recommend them enough. Find your people!

Further Reading

Trans Mission by Alex Bertie

Gender Outlaw by Kate Bornstein

Trans Britain by Christine Burns, MBE

To My Trans Sisters edited by Charlie Craggs

The Gender Games by Juno Dawson

The Transgender Issue by Shon Faye

Transgender Warriors by Leslie Feinberg

The Trans Teen Survival Guide by Fox Fisher and Owl Fisher

What It Feels Like for a Girl by Paris Lees

Trans Like Me by CN Lester

Redefining Realness by Janet Mock

Surpassing Certainty by Janet Mock

Conundrum by Jan Morris

Trans Power by Juno Roche

I'm Afraid of Men by Vivek Shraya

The New Girl by Rhyannon Styles

Born Both by Hida Viloria

Yes, You Are Trans Enough by Mia Violet

There are, of course, an ever-expanding collection of novels featuring trans characters too. Some of them are even written by trans authors such as Alex Gino, Akwaeke Emezi, Fox Benwell, and Meredith Russo.

HAPPY READING!

Glossary

AFAB: Assigned female at birth.

AGENDER: Describes someone with no strong gender identity.

AMAB: Assigned male at birth.

AROMANTIC/ARO: Describes a person who exhibits no or little interest in romantic relationships.

ASEXUAL/ACE: Describes a person who exhibits no or little interest in sexual partnerships.

BINARY: Used to describe a system of two things. In regard to gender, this usually means male and female.

BINDER: A tight-fitting undergarment designed to flatten the chest tissue to create a traditionally masculine silhouette.

BISEXUAL: Describes a person who is attracted to people of two (or more) genders.

BLOCKERS: Informal term for hormonal medication that prevents the onset or effects of sex hormones.

CHASER: An informal term for someone who actively seeks the company of trans partners.

CISGENDER: Describes someone who aligns with the gender they were assigned at birth. This will be the vast majority of people.

DEMISEXUAL: A person who only experiences sexual attraction for people they have a strong emotional connection with.

DRAG QUEEN/DRAG KING: A performer who uses clothes and/or makeup traditionally assigned to a different gender.

ESTROGEN: A hormone that encourages the development of traditionally feminine physical features.

FTM: Female to male. Still used by some medical organizations to describe binary transition.

GAY: Describes a person who is attracted to people of the same gender.

GENDER: A socially constructed notion of what is considered appropriate for people of different sexes. These notions change over geography and points in time.

GENDERQUEER: A spectrum of gender identities that are not exclusively male or female, masculine or feminine.

INTERSEX: A general term for a number of physical conditions whereby an individual's sexual anatomy doesn't match the typical definitions of male or female.

LESBIAN: A woman who is sexually attracted to other women.

MTF: Male to female. Still used by some medical organizations to describe binary transition.

NONBINARY: A spectrum of gender identities that are not exclusively male or female, masculine or feminine. Sometimes used with *trans*, since a nonbinary person may be changing the gender they were assigned at birth.

PACKER: A penis-shaped prosthetic to be worn in the underwear to create a traditionally masculine silhouette.

PANSEXUAL: Describes a person who is attracted to people of any gender identity.

PASSING: When a trans person looks or sounds cisgender in public or online.

PREOP: Sometimes used to describe a trans person who hasn't had any surgeries. A bit outdated now, as many trans people don't want any surgeries.

QUEER: Describes anyone who identifies as something other than cisgender and/or straight.

SEX/SEXUAL ANATOMY: Refers to the five characteristics of physical sex pertaining to reproduction: genetics, hormones, inner and outer genitalia, and the gonads (ovaries and testes).

TESTOSTERONE: A hormone that encourages the development of traditionally masculine physical features.

TRANSAMOROUS: Describes a person who is romantically or sexually attracted to trans people.

TRANSGENDER: Describes anyone changing their gender from the one they were assigned at birth.

TRANSSEXUAL: A more specific term describing those who wish to alter any element of their sexual anatomy.

TRANSVESTITE: Someone who wears clothing or makeup traditionally assigned to another gender.

TRAP: A slur that suggests trans people may fool potential sexual partners.

TUCKING: The process of "tucking away" a penis and scrotum to produce a traditionally feminine silhouette. This can be done with tight underwear or body tape.

References

"Caitlyn Jenner Talks Transition And New Life." *Today Show*, September 9, 2015. YouTube video, 8:24. https://www.youtube.com/watch?v=xFhV7-lEPc0.

"PEOPLE & Oprah Exclusive: The Pregnant Man Speaks Out." *People*, April 2, 2008. https://people.com/tv/people-oprah-exclusive-the-pregnant-man -speaks-out/.

Bergado, Gabe. "Indya Moore's Young Hollywood 2019 Interview on the Groundbreaking Power of *Pose* and the Need for Trans Representation Free from Oppression." *Teen Vogue*, February 7, 2019. https://www.teenvogue.com/ story/indya-moore-young-hollywood-2019.

Bertie, Alex. "I Feel Fake: Trans Advice." January 4, 2018. YouTube video, 6:25. https://www.youtube.com/watch?v=5oDOc7LJgYc.

Casey, Alex. "Georgina Beyer Still Has a Fire in Her Belly." *The Spinoff*, February 14, 2018. https://thespinoff.co.nz/society/14-02-2018/georgina-beyer-still-has -a-fire-in-her-belly/.

Holdom, Ayla. "Ayla Holdom Is the Only Female Helicopter Pilot on the UK Police Force, but She's Used to Breaking Barriers." *Bustle*, June 5, 2018. https://www. bustle.com/p/ayla-holdom-is-the-only-female-helicopter-pilot-on-the-uk -police-force-but-shes-used-to-breaking-barriers-9272426.

Mocarski, Richard, Sim Butler, Betsy Emmons, and Rachael Smallwood. "'A Different Kind of Man': Mediated Transgendered Subjectivity, Chaz Bono on *Dancing*

With the Stars." Journal of Communication Inquiry 37, no. 3 (July 2013): 249–64. https://doi.org/10.1177/0196859913489572.

Moore, Elliott. "Kye Allums Discusses His Personal History as a Transgender Athlete." GLAAD, February 19, 2013. https://www.glaad.org/blog/kye-allums-discusses-his-personal-history-transgender-athlete.

Odiele, Hanne Gaby. "Fashion Model Hanne Gaby Odiele Discloses She Is Intersex." InterACT, January 23, 2017. https://interactadvocates.org/our-advocacy/intersex-media/hanne/#story.

Phillips, Jessica. "Shane Ortega on his Lowest Moment." *GQ*, February 3, 2019. https://www.gq-magazine.co.uk/article/shane-ortega-on-his-lowest-moment.

Romano, Tricia. "Laverne Cox: I Absolutely Consider Myself a Feminist." *Dame*, June 1, 2014. https://www.damemagazine.com/2014/06/01/laverne-cox-i-absolutely-consider-myself-feminist/.

Tobin, Lucy. "Munroe Bergdorf: 'People Wouldn't Go over to Someone's Mother and Ask about Their Labia but They're Happy to Come over to a Trans Person and Ask about Their Genitals." *Evening Standard*, June 5, 2014. https://www.standard.co.uk/lifestyle/london-life/munroe-bergdorf-people-wouldn-t-go-over-to-someone-s-mother-and-ask-about-their-labia-but-they-re-9491573.html.

Wong, Curtis M. "'Billions' Will Make TV History With Gender Non-Conforming Star." *Huffington Post*, December 16, 2016. https://www.huffingtonpost.com.au/entry/billions-gender-nonbinary-character_n_58531cf5e4b08debb78842cb.

Index

Acknowledgments

First up, a huge thank you to *everyone* who selflessly contributed to this book—your kindness and wisdom will hopefully help a vast array of young people better get to grips with their gender. Special praise goes to Soofiya for bringing my words to life with such glorious illustrations.

Thank you to Liza Wilde, who so thoughtfully edited this book, and extra thanks to editorial assistant Halimah Manan for their super smart insights too.

Thank you also to Hot Key Books—especially Emma Matthewson and Jenny Jacoby—for helping to bridge this title and *This Book Is Gay* so effortlessly. What a striking pair they make!

Thanks—as ever—to everyone at my agency: Sallyanne Sweeney and the whole gang.

About the Author

Juno Dawson is a bestselling novelist, screenwriter, journalist, and a columnist for *Attitude* magazine. Her writing has appeared in *Glamour*, *The Pool*, *Dazed*, and the *Guardian*. She has appeared on *Pointless Celebrities*, *BBC Women's Hour*, *Front Row*, ITV News, Channel 5 News, *This Morning*, and *Newsnight*.

Juno's books include the global bestsellers, *This Book Is Gay* and *Clean*. She won the 2020 YA Book Prize for *Meat Market*. She also writes for television and has multiple shows in development both in the United Kingdom and in the United States. An occasional actress and model, Juno had a cameo in the BBC's *I May Destroy You* (2020) and was the face of the Jecca Cosmetics Play Pots campaign.

Juno grew up in West Yorkshire, writing imaginary episodes of *Doctor Who*. She later turned her talent to journalism, interviewing luminaries such as Steps and Atomic Kitten, before writing a weekly column in a Brighton newspaper.

Juno lives in Brighton. She is a part of the queer cabaret collective known as Club Silencio. In 2014, Juno became a School Role Model for the charity Stonewall.

FIREreads

#getbooklit

Your hub for the hottest young adult books!

Visit us online and sign up for our
newsletter at FIREreads.com

 @sourcebooksfire

 sourcebooksfire

 firereads.tumblr.com